T0068193

ADONAI
SPOKEN WORDS ...
GRAFTED IN

MIA LANDAZURI-WEEMS

GOY

גוי

WestBow
PRESS®
A DIVISION OF THOMAS NELSON
& ZONDERVAN

WestBow Press books may be ordered through booksellers or by contacting:

WestBow Press
A Division of Thomas Nelson & Zondervan
1663 Liberty Drive
Bloomington, IN 47403
www.westbowpress.com
1 (866) 928-1240

ISBN: 978-1-5127-7466-5 (sc)
ISBN: 978-1-5127-7468-9 (hc)
ISBN: 978-1-5127-7467-2 (e)

Library of Congress Control Number: 2017901771

Print information available on the last page.

WestBow Press rev. date: 6/23/2017

SWEET SHALOM & THANK YOU...

First to the One and only One ...The Father Adonai and the love of my Life Yeshua, Jesus.... my King, thank you for coming to us, living among us & dwelling with us. Your great sacrifice is carved in our hearts forever.

Thank you for the human gift given ... the Love of my husband whose heart adores You, follows You in truth and simpleness, as You whispered once, he has My heart.

Thank you for the gift to be a mom to my only son whom I adore. Who chose to be a guardian for the freedom of this beautiful land. A heart predestined to be a warrior, not only for the Navy, but also the Army of God, I Pray.

Thank you for giving me 3 daughters when I lost hope of having any of my own.

Thank you, dear Dad and Mom you were born to serve Adonai, and in His care, you are.

My dear Rabbi Hevia and family for your teachings and dedication that brought me one step closer to Him.

My Adopted Dad, Rabbi Zzyzx and Kathy, thank you for being a light in my life.

My second mom... the one who open the door of her heart. An inspiration of courage and determination to "move these writings forward". My beloved and sweet Peggy J. B.

Martha, my dear friend, whom witnessed my transformation when I spoke to her about the place I call unknown, you believed in me and we believed in Him together.

The reason why I kept the original writings.... Pastor Koffi. One day, he said, do not throw away those for they will be of much value.

Especially, my shalom to the smallest Messianic tribe in the world, "The Movie Bunch". As we diligently wait for the Sabbath, a meeting with the Holy One.

My family far away and friends and all the hands that supported me throughout my own walk ...as my ancestors did....in the howling desert under the stars.

A journey to the promised land, shadowed by the Pillar of Fire and the Great Cloud.

Also a special thanks and credit for the creation of the book cover by Chris Shuster, who's talent and expertise brought to life the inspired vision given to me from the Lord.

TABLE OF CONTENTS

Foreword ix

Chapter 1 My Heart 1
  ✡ With A Kiss My Love 3
  ✡ Revive Me Oh Lord 6
  ✡ Living God 8
  ✡ People Of Mine...10
  ✡ Tears 12

Chapter 2 Law – Torah - Grace 15
  ✡ A Sorrows Knight 17
  ✡ My Name – Hashem...22
  ✡ I Am the Cross Barer...26
  ✡ Anokhi 29
  ✡ False Gods..35

Chapter 3 Love – Joy – Shalom 43
  ✡ In My Arms, You Are...45
  ✡ The Lord of the Sabbath 51
  ✡ Stitch by Stitch...54
  ✡ The Wedding Day 65
  ✡ The Waiting..70

Chapter 4 Warnings 75
  ✡ Yeshua the Great Angel 77
  ✡ The Watchman of the Bride 80
  ✡ Breath....... I Am Here 83
  ✡ Deny Yourself to Receive 86
  ✡ Do Not Take Me With You 89

Chapter 5 Warfare...97
  ✡ I Was Made To Save.. 98
  ✡ I AM the Father's Lion... I AM the Father's
    Lamb...103
  ✡ Not of This World...108
  ✡ To The Warrior 114
  ✡ In the Midst of the Battle.................................... 119

Chapter 6 His Expectations - Gavah 123
  ✡ His Expectations...125
  ✡ A Change of Heart 133
  ✡ Walk My Walk …..137
  ✡ Face to Face 139
  ✡ Truth... Love... Hope 143

Chapter 7 Rest.. 147
  ✡ I Am the God Who Sees 149
  ✡ My Heart Never Left..154
  ✡ Everlasting El Olam – Elohim.............................158
  ✡ Trials of Love, Trials of Faith 161
  ✡ AT the End of the Road 165

A Prayer from the Writer 169

FOREWORD

IT IS NOT ABOUT THE WRITER ....IT IS ALL
ABOUT THE AUTHOR.

I am only a hand that follows Adonai's command... only able
to write when He speaks in my heart, when He takes me to a
place I call "the unknown".

A place where I dwell in Him, under my tallit with my fingers
trapped in the tzizith.

A place where my eyes are closed as I feel my hand moving by
His command along with my heart beat, tears & His Spoken
Words and a heartbeat of His own.

At times my hand will stop, as He is quiet in my heart, then
I am back to only intercede and cry out to Him for mercy,
forgiveness, and love.

At the beginning were few words as you will read in the first
chapter. I wrote expressing my love and this strange feeling to
write that I never felt before.

Later, I heard His voice saying it's time to write, especially in
the middle of the night.... on the Sabbath day, until one day He

said from now on there will be two writings, your questions, and My answers. His spoken words became scrolls and for hours I would remain in the unknown.

A few drawings came along & a few musical notes as well as I would cry out many times, Father I do not know how to write or paint or play .... Oh, this fire that you have placed in me. HE Would whisper, "Just close your eyes and trust in ME" ...and so I did learn to trust HIM and the unknown.

As you will see, in the original writings, there are lines between the words.... that is the time when my hand learned to stop moving as He has stopped speaking, then pauses, so I translate that to you into dots.... a time to pause... and breathe… and take in His message and Love.

Who I was and who I Have become is the story of a lost shy soul that diligently seeks for His love. In great times of need and trouble while in my own wilderness, under the howling desert, the great heat burning my soul, my sins, the stars, under my own sukkah mourning for the God of the Hebrews, my people all Jew and Gentile.

In my childhood, as my family recalls, I was there in the "unknown" twisted in the embrace of my blanket and my fingers wrapped in the fringes I would be found speaking a word over and over and over again, louder, and louder, even in the middle of the night, they will have to wake me up. That word was … Goy! Which in my native language has no meaning but in the heavenly language and ancient Hebrew the word "goy" means "nation". In the Torah, *goy* and its variants appear over 550 times in reference to Israelites and to Gentile nations.

Was I pre destined to be part of the army of our God? Like many of us that were silent and now we have a voice, were blind and now we can see. We can hear & we are ready to follow the King and His army to save the ones that are lost ...as we also were once. Who I was or who I have become means little as it really is all about the Author and His love story...... The Greatest love story between the human heart and the Holy One of Israel.

@nce you have burnt me
than you have shut burnt me
clem your hand burnt me) rathe than
clmy thru the past

I ull tame no nuuy ta
I have show you du
lore or ull light
again & again will
the vuy end ___ I ull
be looiuy for your returned
heart to take you to the tastu
& plead m groat muuy ___

you ment unduhme &
cicuueue four homut
FOR I walked with
you ___ I' am with
I' have to have you

my Heart is yours
my love is yours
my shield is yours
my word is yours
my source is yours
but I AM the
great I AM Holy---ADONAT
EHM

My beloved Son yeshua
He is Holy
only have His Holiness you will be
worthy of my FORGIVEN--- only have Him
mercy will Come ---- As love As you
call His name with Adoration & Reverence
I will be the God who
forgives

xiii

CHAPTER 1

My Heart

With A Kiss My Love

I lift my hands to the heavens.... With a kiss to you My Lord
as I open my eyes and realize.......
it is Your love... I am alive......!

It is because my deepest love....I choose
to obey. I close my heart &
close my eyes to the world as I, with Your Holy Spirit,
choose to crucify the flesh......and let sin go by.
It is because, my deepest love, ... I can't choose to hurt You....
send tears...to my Father in heaven.....pierce Your
love with sadness.....rather than a kiss.

A thousand times by day....by night....
I fight... I choose not to sin.
not because you are my King...YHVH ...
not by fear ...because You are mighty...
not because the miracles given...
not because Torah...
Are not my failures from the past who led
me to redemption through Yeshua?
Is not by knowledge.... I know Your power is in Him.

I choose not to sin......
because .... I love You.... I love You
because You first loved me and I don't want to hurt You......
because Your hope is in me.... You trust in me.......
because my kisses I need You to receive.

3

Why would I choose to make You sad once more....
when by blindness.....I did in the past?
Why would I choose to make You cry.....with tears of sadness?
when, by Your mercy, my own tears, You
heal with love and kindness?

Why would I choose to let go of Your
hand and break Your heart
when by Your endless love was I rescued once from the death
and revived by the touch of Your holy hand.....?

Why would I choose to stain my tallit with sin..
when, by Your purity, my heart is wrapped around and with a
kiss my fingers in the tzitzit trapped as I lose myself in prayer?

Holy Sabbath, that brings the scrolls, that dance around us
with a kiss my lips are fulfilled with Your word
as we cross the door to the heavens.
Mezuzah, with a kiss I renew my love to You and
for that moment to the heavens belong....
as my lips cry out like the broken sound of the shofars,
the broken sound of my sin, as I bend my will
to Yours, knowing that nothing's more whole to You than a
broken sound, a broken heart that brings a kiss from above.
Oh the sorrow, the deepest sadness, the misery of this heart…
if knowingly I fail You, my love,
my kisses waist away by my sin.
Agony by day and by night......to live my days
knowing that I choose to go back to death.
Atonement is my only hope, when I was saved at the cross.

This is why I praise You,
this is why I worship You,
the reason why I lift my hands to heavens with a kiss,
because I love You.

Why do I run to You?
why do I blow the shofar calling You,
why do I have joy, peace, and hope?
Because I choose to fight sin and rejoice in
what You have given me to be free.

You gave me the chance to be redeemed.
You gave me a chance to show You my love through the fight.
You gave me a chance to receive Your Shalom.
You gave me a chance to show You my endless love.
And with a kiss, sealed my covenant of love.
For an eternity, my kisses are Yours.

~ Goy ~

Revive Me Oh Lord

In the quietness of the heart our souls rejoice.
Silence has a voice that whispers our love.
Our heart cries out with every beat calling You Lord.
Revive me that the loneliness will be fulfilled with grace.
Stillness is the reassurance of Your love in this heart of Yours.

Revive my soul, the waited Sabbath it is upon.
Open Thou my eyes to see the light of my life,
my Creator, my King.
Revive me from the depths of my sleep.
The Sabbath, like the morning breeze, is here...
wash me thoroughly with the mist of Your peace...
let Your grace wake me so to proclaim Your holy name.

You mighty and sweet Creator of day and night...
open thou my eyes when by Your command the
night rolls away to welcome the morning light.
Revive me in the midst of the morning by Your kindness...
another day, another giving chance for love.

Oh' sweet quietness .... be still, be still.
Revive me oh my Lord.
Open thou my lips oh' God of the beginning
Elohay Kedem.
Open Thou this heart to beat that I shall
not have other gods before You.
Revive our souls, anoint us all,

with few notes, few steps, few words to
glorify before the glory of the King.

Revive me not from the depths if Thy
commands I will not obey.
Revive me not if Your name is not proclaimed
with reverence and grace.
Revive not this soul if the battle in Your name won't be won.

Leave me in loneliness if I should ever
doubt of Your great love.
Revive me not if with every breath this heart
takes is not humble and thankful for Thee...
Save me and I am alive.

With mercy and supplication, I pray to You, oh' my King,
that my eyes will only see You, my heart will only follow You.
Through me Your hands will hold the ones in need,
my lips will be sealed and still
waiting for the time You have prepared for me.

Until then, revive me Oh Lord.
Command my eyes lids to close and rest in peace
until the next Sabbath is here,
until, in the midst of the morning, by Your grace
another day, another giving chance
and forever dwell in Thee.

~ Goy ~

Living God

Living, breathing,
only by Your grace.
Not living from the flesh, but from Your holy name.
Not breathing from the air, but from Your everlasting breath.
Not shining by the light, but by Your divine presence.
Only alive by the love of the living God.

El, Elohim, Adonai has spoken.
We are Your work, Your perfection made flesh.
This earth, this universe, creation,
every season with a reason by Your wisdom.
Every creature with a purpose by Your
knowledge.
Our living God fills our world, fills our
souls with His perfection, made love, to comfort us all.
"I and I alone " as you said.
Your spirit, living in Your ancient walls.
Your presence, found when we pass the gates of praise,
gates open to surrender and love.

Your fullness found in Your fire made word.
Word to fulfill the covenant of the living God, the book of life.
Eternal....living ....Father and Son...
living in You will prevent dyeing.
Edifying will open the gate to dwelling.
Supplication the path to my Creator.
Rebuilding of our life's, rebuilding of our
souls only if rebuilding the

temple for the last time.
Temple of our hearts and You living in us.
Temple living in the dwelling land,
land waiting for its King to dwell forever,
waiting for His people to surrender to the
power of the sound...of the great shofar, to the
living God, the living Son.
Your name has the power to save.
Your name, in the midst, allowing us to
close our eyes, lie down in peace and rise up in Thee.
Your holy name, the Most High.
Your glory carved in every soul, every mountain, every
ocean, every pasture, all the heavens and all the stars.
Every living cell is carved and is alive
by the grace of the living God.
Without You, no life,
You and only You,
the Almighty, I Am.

The loving Father, the perfect love to all,
Your beautiful face shining on us from heaven,
Your heart surrounding us in earth.

Only alive, breathing and living
only until Thy Majesty will descend to us below.
Until then, Thy Lord,
living by Thy love shall be
looking at Your throne,
only alive by my heart beating for the living God.

~ Goy~

People Of Mine

Within my soul, oh sweet Lord, feeling their hearts in mine.
People of mine that I belong to,
people of mine that make this heart cry
out for their past and for their God.

Is that lonely star in the dark sky, shining at my eyes? Tears
fall, longing for the King's heart and the promised land.
El Shaddai, God of mine, God of all.
What is this call, who are these people of mine,
dwelling between Your heart and mine?

Inside I live their lives as a write.
I know their hearts, I cry their tears, carrying
their tambourines in my heart.
Their howling desert, I'm longing for…
I know their love for the living God, they
mourn and rejoice …… dwelling love!

People of my heart, as I write of their obedience to I Am,

not seeing You, not touching You ….but
knowing Father, Spirit & Son.
Spoken words echo in their hearts, words
from their almighty God.
A living temple of hearts and tribes dwelling for El Shaddai.

Doubt and disobedience becomes a journey of endless miles.
From the desert to this heart to this night

as they walk, as I write,
as their lives unfold in my own scrolls
within their silence guiding, learning,
doubting, dancing, praising.
People of mine hunted by the angels of the dark.
People of mine by their God's grace, seeing
miracles, receiving commandments,
knowing that the fire of their only God will never die.

This heart of mine longing for the mountain of
the Lord, the greatness of His presence.....
longing for the Shepherd's heart, their goats, lambs, their land
longing for the Temple. This heart has 7 chambers.
This heart dressed with a tallit, purples and whites
longing for the Sabbath mystery and majesty of the Divine.
This guiding force blending our hearts with...the great I Am.

Who I was, who I am, who I have become
as I write my soul, my love, my own
scrolls as the people of the Lord
I am alive. I am alive for You Adonai,

Only for You, King of the people of mine.
Only for the Father.…. Holy Spirit and
Yeshua, Jesus the King Son.
Only for Your glory, holy, holy One.
Only for the fire of the living God that will never die.

~ Goy ~

Tears

Tears of love, Adonai, my love.
I can feel Your tears my Lord.
I can feel Your sadness like drops of blood.
Like violins playing Your heart's songs,
playing Your sweet voice.

Eli, Eli, Tears of Your sadness, inside me.
Is this how You feel? So, sad. I despair,
my heart fades, Adonai, Adonai!
Tears of human souls running from a "night of broken glass".
A night that will break Your heart, a dark night.

Tears that eco sadness, human crying.
An agony without hope.
Ashes like clouds in the sky.
Clouds trying to find their loved ones
one more time, one more time.
Cold hearts, winter nights,
endless days and nights, like icicles cold and sharp.
Snowflakes fall like heavenly kindness,
Touching kisses to calm their tears of sadness.

Trains filled with shining stars. Tracks with
no hope, only love trapped within.
Tears with questions … what have we done?
We are the chosen ones. Stop, mercy, stop!

Beautiful Star that can't glide. The only
way to survive.....hide in the dark.
Hunger is the price, stripes and a star is their mark.

Tears from heaven, when let me die becomes the cry.
Silence becomes new language, surrender becomes hope.
Teary eyes that learn to speak with
violins crying for the meek.
Playing for every beautiful child...
playing for every old heart....
playing for every ghetto....for every camp.....
Playing for the ones that will survive ...Shoah.

Tears of hope, strings of love.
The Star will always shine, an eternal light.
Shabbat will survive evil hearts.

Adonai Eloheinu....The Lord is our God.
Star of David ...The world's light.
Tears of blood, tears of sorrow, tears of horror no more.
Tears of hope, tears of joy, tears of kindness. Shalom! Shalom!
Tears....Strings... Ashes…... Stars.......all in our Lord's Heart.
All shadowed by the covenant of love.
All shadowed by the Dove of Peace, the Dove of Love.
The dove that lives in our hearts, Adonai, Adonai.

~ Goy ~

CHAPTER 2

Law — Torah - Grace

A Sorrows Knight

Among you who is the righteous one?
Who is the one who goes to the left or the right?

There are none...they cover their heads and
bow down to Me with unclean hearts.

Then who is the righteous one, the one
who goes to the left or the right?

Do not try to be righteous but first remain in My law.
Do not try in My name to judge or go left or right
for to My eyes there is none left or right.

For I see your hearts that change like the waters that I once
walked, hearts like the currents change high and low.

They can't be still like the storm that I once calmed.

Hearts like the great winds that I Am in control of.

Winds that go about destroying souls,
winds that cannot be still, like your hearts
that cannot find peace and calm.

Righteous men, there are none, My grace will not make
you right. The affliction of their souls as they battle for
righteousness will never cease for only through Me,
Yeshua, Jesus is the only way to righteousness.

Lost in Me you should live.

Lost in My dwelling holiness you should
be. Breathing through Me,
Yeshua Jesus, your King...grace will come.

Remain in Me.

Torah was given to your fathers; their
hearts were tested with fire...
through fire they were able to receive
the word of the Great Father.
Word that is spoken with righteousness of the heart...
It came to pass...it came to life...it came to power,
Then it came to fade in the heart of the unrighteous.

The word is Me, Yeshua, Jesus...and I Am
in the one who gave you the Torah.
Torah fell into evil hands that would use it to conquer ...that
use My name to create false power... That use My word to
kill and destroy...they use My word to deny Me, their King.

I Am the King who came to bring salvation to
the world, the only one who is the trusted and
righteous unto you below for I Am holy.

Until that day... The word of the Creator
is to be carried in your hearts.

The unjust, prideful, self-righteous,
jealous, stubborn of heart...
will be judged even if My word is in their mouth.

Righteousness is in Me, only lived when I see
purity ...that is rooted in your hearts...
purity of heart that remains still... always still like
the waters that I commanded to be in peace.

Righteousness is the purity that I see when
your heart is steadfast even in the midst of
the storm, the storm that I will call
upon when I see you following Me, rather
than going back to the past.

Righteousness, it is to Me, when I see that
you receive the Fathers spoken words in your
heart with reverence and humbleness.

A gift given not for your glory and self-righteousness
among others, but for your own simpleness and truth.

Truth that is written in the scrolls with no change,
with no change to the right or to the left, each
letter counted one by one to fulfill My Father's
commands and the wonders of great Adonai.
I Am the word of God ...I Am Yeshua, Jesus, the living Torah.

I will come seeking for the purity of
the holy word of your hearts...
I Am blessing you.

For the ones that use the word of God for self-righteousness, I
will destroy. For the knowledge of the word will not save you.

For the holy word of Adonai is a sword that will condemn
the self-righteousness of the ones who speak to the
crowd's... for the ones who cry out their denial at the wall
of My beloved land Jerusalem...whether you're a priest
or a king or a poor man, I will destroy the wicked.

It is by faith in Me and repentance unto My word
that will save you.

Before anything..... Come to Me, Yeshua, the King.
Before you speak about the wonders of
great Adonai, come to Me.
Before you come to the sacred scrolls, come to Me.
I will fulfill your heart with the purity
that you need to receive...
before your request, come to Me.

I will cleanse your heart so the purity of your request
will be heard in the Father's heart as a love song.

Yes My beloved…. purity is the love song that will bring
you closer to My holiness and My righteousness.
For purity dwells in kindness...
kindness dwells in peace...

Peace dwells in Me...

and I, Yeshua Hamaschiack, Sar Shalom, dwells in
righteousness of the One above, great Adonai Tzevaot.

(AND I, JESUS THE CHRIST, PRINCE OF PEACE,
DWELLS IN RIGHTEOUSNESS OF THE ONE
ABOVE, THE GREAT LORD OF HOSTS.)

Come to Me, says the Lord, come to Me.

My Name — Hashem

Hashem, The Name.

As I ask you my Lord, the pain I feel when I hear Your
name not proclaimed with reverence and respect.

So lightly spoken.

How to explain the beauty of Your name?

Suddenly I feel the breeze… Your spoken words, whispering.

My holy name …it is like the wind…. do
not know where it comes from….
My name is tender and powerful, eternal, Hashem!

My name has no name, sacred and holy.
My name, says the Lord, has the sounds
of love, has the sounds of grace.
Listen to the wind, listen to the heart.

My name it is known to you, mystery of Hashem.
A breath of grace…. that made man.

My name comes from the depths of heaven….
where the majesty and mystery of My love dwells.

My name....it is joy.... as it is peace....
My name.... It is love that restores.... a gift to humanity...
My name.... can feel and touch....
My name .... can hear and cry....
My name .... will save and condemn........!

My name it is the breeze from above.... in
the midst of creation.... I Am.....
My name will rise up.... and calm the rising waters....
listen to your heart.... listen to the wind .... for ...I Am.

My name is in the dark as it is in the light...
it heals and strikes.
a gift from .... Hashem....the breath of life.

To pronounce My name......with
reverence...grace and holiness....
for .... I Am .... your salvation......human kind.
For... I Am ...Yeshua ...Jesus...the King
Son...the Giver of life and death.

As you announce My name.... bow down
to Me for.... I Am who I Am...
Adonai eternal.

My holy name to be separated.... from your humanness.
Announce My love.... but rather be dead ...if
My name with holiness is not said.
Cut off your tongue.... before you call My name in vain.

23

Cover your head when My name it is to be proclaimed...
for miracles will come.... if your spoken
words are to exalt My name.

Listen to the wind ...listen to the heart...!

My holy name sprinkles this earth...with joy and love...
in the morning dew, in the breath at night.

My name shines in every star....

My name is on My word .... as it is in your hands tonight....

Bow-down to Me.....with grace.... proclaim My name....
to please the sacrifice of love.... I made....
to please the One above all.
The great ...I Am.

My blessings are yours ...My love...My child...
as you speak My name....it will fulfill
you ...with holiness and grace....
grace given to you, so to teach others....
so that their own words
will not condemn them.... if My holy
name it is not proclaimed....
With love and grace......

Listen to the wind.... listen to the heart......for I Am.

I Am your King.... you are My child......
Do not mix My holiness ...with humanness......

Worship My name ......in the name of praise....
call upon My name with adoration.... but not in vain.......

listen to the wind.... listen to the heart.......
for My holy name is there....

whispering My love to you.... whispering
My peace and joy ....to you......
My love ...My child......!

I Am the Cross Barer

Write through me, my beloved Yeshua, tell me about the cross
so, that I may understand what you feel.

I Am... Yeshua the cross carrier.... the
cross barer.... the sin breaker.

Write and write a word tonight...
The cross... the cross... the cross... (quiet- sigh)

A symbol of love.... a symbol of hate...
I carried .... I walked with it...
as they hated Me.....as they loved Me.

Every step I had to take.......upon....... (quiet...sigh)
every sin was carried ......on the cross.......

your sin .... I took upon the hills.

As I walked....it was the weight of your
sin... I carried with Me...
for the weight of the cross ...was not.

My flesh was whole...for it was for your sin...
that the flesh had to be exposed....to great pain...and sorrow.

The cross was chosen....by the one Creator above all.
As a sign of great love......
for it was the cause of human sin...the pain and sorrow...
I took upon the hills.

In obedience to the One above all...
great Adonai...My Father....
every nail that on Me was....
had the weight of your denial.

Had the weight of your disobedience...
for the nail was not the cause of pain on Me...
the pain was the weight of your sin.

A human crown was engraved on My flesh…
as a sign of all your sorrows.

I Am Yeshua Jesus .... the sin breaker...
I Am... the one who was sent .... the one
you love ...the one you hate.

Hate is not in Me.... hate it is not from the cross…
hate comes from sin......sin you chose to carry......in you.

Hate that you .... will not be able to
bear....it will nail your peace...
only if you choose to crucify the flesh....
you will be able to be free.

My blood .... covers all creation.......saves all creation.

Only through Me ...Yeshua Hamaschiack......
The Son of the great Creator........you will find eagle wings.

For I Am ...the way to the great Father......

For I Am... the way beyond the cross.......

I Am the way to eternal shalom.

I will come to set you free.... believe in Me....
believe in the freedom of sin...

Covered by My blood you will be able
to breath....and be alive.

My great love.... the cross.... life ... death ....
were all written in the heavens...

Since the beginning of time...
in all the stars....in all creation.... every cell is alive...
by the grace and love of the great Creator...

Adonai and Yeshua the king Son...
The Cross carrier.... The Cross barer.... of all human kind.

Anokhi

Anokhi
Breathe that.... I Am..... Anokhi....the God of all...

Anokhi....I Am the will...the power....
I Am the God who breathes.... creates.... judges....
I Am the God who's will ...will prevail.

My land and My people.... are surrounded
by the enemy's fire....
fire surrounding the 12 gates.... as it was once in the past....
the enemy gathers....as one....to destroy and control....
what is Mine…..

You, My people......My beloved bride....M y Jerusalem.

The enemy does not know the wrath of.... Anokhi…. God....
the wrath of all the heavens will come.

Fierce angels I will send....to destroy for the last time....
My angels are gathered by the 12 gates.

Many refuse to believe in Me.....their only Creator.
The breath who gave them life....and will give them death....
for they don't understand.... My great power....
for they don't understand.... My great destruction....
they don't know the fierce wrath of great Adonai......Anokhi.

Be aware.... for the one dark angel.... He
knows Me.... He fears Me....!!
He knows the season.... when I will come....
he knows of his own hour and end ...until
then he comes to you....
to devour you....to destroy you.

He knows that only through your weakness he can survive......
he knows that only through faith in My son Yeshua....
you will have eternal life and he will perish forever.

For he has dwelt and submitted to My
Beloved Son's presence in
the wilderness.... forty days and nights...

for he knows the Son of great Anokhi....
Yeshua, Elohim Chayim...the living God...

My breath will consume it all!

I.....will send My angels....as a warning.
Finally, you, My beloved bride will see...
the mysteries of all the heavens come to your life....
your eyes will witness.... the times.... of the great wrath....
for great faith, I see in your hearts...!!

Be strong!!.......Your eyes must remain
on My son, Yeshua, Jesus...
through Him is the only way that you...My fragile creatures....
will be able to witness the end of times.... and not die.

Only the faith you are showing Me will able you to
witness My great power.
Only the simpleness in your heart.... will allow
you to see the power of My heart.

The purity in you.... will be the covering....
then your eyes will witness the heavens come to life......
great angels.... great battles.

Behold.... the enemy you will see....come to face...

Ani....Ani...Ani....I will be in you....
I will protect you.
behold.... the last...warnings.

Behold.... before Me....
I will allow you to see the end....be strong.

Your own people ...you will see walking
towards the light of My glory.
Your own people ...you will see walking....
towards the end...the dark.
Nothing.... will I change then...
dark will be consumed by the dark....
eternal flame...dying life.
Light will be consumed by My eternal glory.... forever life.

I Am choosing you....to walk in a time ...where you will see...
the beginning of life....
I Am choosing you to witness.... the great battle....

the great dance by My side.
My beloved .... your king, Yeshua...will return....
To fulfill My promises.... for He is My
word.... writing in the scrolls.

In the midst of the battle ...He will gather you....
His love and great mercy will carry you.

Be prepared....be aware....be in awe!!
Be in reverence...sanctify your self's.

Ani...Ani ...Ani...!!
Be of a pure heart....be of a strong heart....
be of a truthful heart...be of a clean heart.......
this is the only way .... for the few ...that will remain....
to survive what is to come....
witness the word come to life!
Be of a mighty heart.... for you to be
able to bear....and not die.
My great wonders...as your fore fathers
did.... Noah....Mosses...
for they witnessed My wrath that did destroy the wicked......
for they bore the law...and in My presence, they are alive....
be strong...do not be afraid.
I....great Anokhi....I Am choosing you...
I Am giving you revelation for what is to come...
to be prepared....to know more about Me.

Save others.... through love....
make them strong.... make them whole....

prepare them for the way of glory.

Adonai your God has spoken!
My fire will burn the wicked forever!

My fire will protect My bride...I will
surround you and My land....
My light will be guiding you....
none of your hairs will be touched for
your body will be glorified.
You will see My Beloved Son's return .... with all His glory...!
His angels...will come ....in accord
with My plan and command.

All the heavens......all the angels....in one
to put to death.... the dark angel...the one
who calls himself the king of all darkness.
The one who in the light of My love once was....
the one who in My fire will have a dying life......forever.

I Anokhi....the great... I Am...
One angel, for each of you, I have created.......to protect.
My humble ...faithful .... beautiful.... yet.... fragile creation....
I believe in you......My love, it is yours.

I Am Yeshua, Jesus ...your guardian angel......
I will return to you...you will see Me.

The great dance...the final day.... the great beginning....
the great reward…. the great temple!

A place on the Father's throne....
next to Me you will be.... My bride...Jerusalem....
all peace...all love will be yours.... eternal shalom.

The word will be fulfilled.... from beginning to end....
from your hearts....to Mine.

I, Yeshua the king Son......I will.... I will....
present you... In My arms....to the Father with great joy......!!

Each of you will be on the throne....
In My arms as an offering of love......
in My arms as a seal.... for the book of life.......!

False Gods

Until I came.... until I came.
I came to save, not to destroy.
I came in the name of the greatest love....
The love of your creator.

Until I came...... to be with man....be born from man....
to bring My Father's command for the last time...
For a time, it is of your world.... for your
God, great Adonai, time is not.

I came to love, to give you a living life....
for you to eat, from the palm of My hand, be fed....
with teachings of love.

Until I came...until I came......(sigh).

Man, lost in sin .... worshiping false gods.... that man made...
gods that destroy.... My Father's creation......
gods that call you ...to worship what shines, silver, and gold...
gods that want your souls....to be
transformed to what they are....
the dark!

These gods will not save you from the gates of fire.
For they belong to the place that the Father
created for the angels of dark.

For it is evil who has created the gods
you worship and praise....
out of wickedness.
Dead gods without a heart....with no love....
no compassion....no law....
for they have a covenant with sin.
They rejoice and dwell in the
perdition of your human souls.

Know My heart ....and answer Me....
which of your gods has a breath that creates life?
Which of your gods will cover you as
you walk in the desert under the

stars as the pillar of fire and the great cloud?

Which of your gods will command the
oceans part for you to cross into the
promised land?

Which of your gods will call upon an
army of angels to rush to you in
times of need?

Which of your false gods can add a minute to your life,
stop or bring to life your human heart?

Which of your gods will leave their wicked thrones...
to come to you and carry the sins of the world?

The walk of the cross....to die...
to live....in the name of love!

And so, I came to (sighs)....to save you
from the gods of the past....
gods that were dead....and you choose to bring them to life.

Your Father in the heavens.... He is your
only God...He is the great judge.
If you choose sin....and choose to dwell in that covenant....
death will be unto you.....
death will be unto you.... I will not
save...I will not save you then.
For My Father's command, I will obey.
Until then......
Shema (listen)...hear My heart.... turn
your back to the wicked.
Turn your back to false gods.... before
your souls are lost forever.
And so, I came to you.... I came to you...
the sacrifice was made!
Yet, nothing has changed, for I see your hearts rejoice with
the pleasures of the flesh.
Blood on your hands......
I see.... the mark of the beast in your hearts......in your eyes....
there is no holiness....in what you worship.
No holiness, the blood of others is upon you.
You who preach in My name and in wickedness dwell.

So, I came ....and so I came to you....
To witness the love of great Adonai....
He sees you from the great throne.... with great compassion...
great sorrow.... great love.

I came to stay in you.... for My spirit ....
I left.... dwelling.... guiding....
always whispering to you.... warning
you.... when you are about to
worship false gods.

I came to stay....so that you will witness
great miracles in faithful hearts.

I came to stay in you through the battle ...of your daily life....
to fulfil the great law.... written in the sacred scrolls....
written in your hearts.

I Am, Yeshua, Jesus....the living God, made man.
The one who lived ...died ....and rose from the dead....
to bring all who will believe from depths
of death unto eternal life.

I will come back on the day....
to be with you, My obedient hearts.

You will see Me....
My reward will exceed all your dreams....
The Father's great love...will bring you to the kingdom
He has prepared for you.

Listen to My whispers of love...when in doubt....
look around.... up and below.... I created all....
My power, it is beyond your understanding....
My love it is greater than the gods you feel for.

When in doubt.... hear the beat of your
own heart.... I Am there....
when in doubt.... look at your being....
I Am there.
When in doubt.... see the creatures of the waters.... the wild....
the air.... I Am there.

When in doubt.... look at the stars.... I know them by name....
as I know your name....
I know of your needs....and desires...
most of all.... when in doubt.... nourish in My word.... My law.

For it was created to protect you from false gods.

Know of My word made love.... for it was written....
For in the beginning I was......and to
the last word I will be there.

Do not be afraid....to be in Me.
Choose the living God...great Adonai....trust ...obey....
be of a brave heart.... have I not already shown you...?

That I ...Yeshua, Jesus...I Am in the Father....
The Father is in Me.... I Am in you.... you are in Me?

Hear oh...shema .... Israel......
none will enter the kingdom.... without the Son....
for in the presence of the Holiest of Hollies none will survive.

And so, I came....in humbleness....in
reverence....to the One above all....
Adonai Sevauot.... Adonai of the beginnings....
The God of what was, is and is to
come.... the everlasting God.

CHAPTER 3

Love — Joy — Shalom

In My Arms, You Are

In My arms, you are My love.
Can you not see.... all around you?
Open your eyes.... see.... That I, Yeshua, your king....

The one you call ....my love....
I Am protecting you.... My angels are all around you....
Watching over you.

Your beloved was sent from Me....do not doubt in him,
for he has My heart....
in time, you will see...the plan I have prepared for you.

Until then ....keep on writing....
do not be afraid....do not go against the light....
even if the darkness you see for such a time.

In Me you should remain My child......
people all around you with arms wide open for you My child....
as a sign that I, Yeshua, the king ...I Am protecting you....
do not be afraid.... come to Me ...run to Me.

In My arms, you are.
My arms are open.... for all My beloved people.

Come to Me.... the time has come...
My father's will .... his promises will be fulfilled.

The word that in you is
fully fulfilled by great Adonai.
From the beginning to the end.... until then...
come to Me, My child.

By the Father's grace....
the King's Son has the capacity to protect all His creation.

The desire of My heart it is to embrace you in My arms...
for you to feel the protection and love of Adonai eternal.
My arms... I stretched out once....at the cross......
at a time that I had to give My own
heart for all human kind....
In the name of love....in sorrow....in great pain.

In redemption....in surrender....to My Father........
For I Am the only way to salvation…..

See the cross...see My arms....as a sign of love.

Love endures all pain......as it departs the flesh....
to become of the Spirit, you must crucify
the flesh in your hearts.

For it is the only way to come to the light....
For it is the only way for you to feel My arms around you.

My arms My child.... never rest......
My arms are.... always open....by your side.......
waiting for you to turn away from sin......and find Me.

you belong to Me........... I Am holy........
You belong to Me.....Yeshua, the King, the redeemer.

You belong to Me.......for I Am the sacrifice
that was poured out once and for all.

My arms cover all the heavens ...all
the stars......and your hearts.

See the birds of the skies.... their wings are open...
ready to embrace another day, another chance.......
with no fear.... for they trust in the power given by their great
Creator....
to leave the ground and fly high above the skies.

Can you see their wings ...? covering their nest....
ready to be fulfilled.... for they know the Father's will.

To protect the gift of a new life.....
how much more then.... would the Father do for you?

With My arms, wide open at the time it had to be done.
I did surrender to Him and took the sin of all human kind....

In the name of love.

See the creatures of the seas
with great peace....

they go about.... dancing in the midst of the waves....
ready to battle the power of the currents...
ready to encounter and defend their loved ones.... for they
know when predators swim around....
they know their own capacity......until
the waters calm.... they go on....
for they trust and know the One who gives life.
For they know their own laws.... they know....
what they were created for....by doing so they bow down to
their Creator.

How much more will My arms.... do for you My child?
The sacrifice was made.......a mind
and a heart you were given.

A mind to choose the plan of salvation...
to know when evil is around.......ready to destroy.
A heart I gave you.... for you to feel My love.
To be embraced by the power of the Father and Son...

A heart and mind.... for you to feel and understand....
the love letters written in the scrolls.

Then you must trust in Me, Yeshua, Jesus your savior.
turn away from the evil in you.... then...

you will see the plan of salvation the Father has prepared
for all his creation and then in My arms you will be.

My arms await for you to come and remain in My shalom.
Shalom that will be with you ...until the last breath.

My arms are in the midst of you...as you sleep and awake....
My arms are in the midst of your battles....

My arms are in the midst of your life....
know the Fathers desires.... His plan .... His commands....

See the word.... feel the word... Live
the word.... obey the word....
For I, Yeshua Hamaschiack, I Am there.

In My arms ...you are.
Your surrender to Me... Your obedience to Me....
discipline from the heart.... will bring you closer to Me.

I will not leave you behind....
I will not forsake you.... My child.
Every time you doubt Me…. Your king.

See the birds of the air.
See the creatures of the seas.
See the shadow of the cross....

You will see....
My arms covering all the heavens all the stars....

For......In My arms.... you are.
For....In My arms …. you will remain.

My arms are the only way.

Truly, truly,
My arms will take you to the place that you belong....
My arms will take you....to the love of great Adonai....
The Creator.

I will take you all…..My beloved......
To My Father.... With arms of an angel......

!! Trust in Me.....believe in Me.....!!!

!!Yeshua Hamaschiack, the Great Angel...!!

The Lord of the Sabbath

The Lord of the Sabbath
I Am the peace…

Yeshua….the Lord of the Sabbath….
I Am…..the rainbow across the sky….
I Am….the truth awakening your eyes.

On the Sabbath….come to Me…..
My peace will reign in your heart….
To find Me….to follow Me …leave your everyday life.

You must…. set yourself apart.
It is My command to obey this very special day.
Can you see the light…. while you strive…?
Can you hear My voice……while you talk…?

Can you feel My heart beat …next to yours?

While you rush…. through your day…
without allowing your heart to stop….
so that My heart beat…. will be the one to guide.

To find rest …. silence in this holy day….it is My command.

How can the rainbow be seen…. after the storm….
If it's colors by My command …call upon you….
And your eyes are looking down…. rather than above…?

Let the sun go down.... let the moon shine....
wait for Me in silence....
I Am coming to love.... the Sabbath it is upon.

Your work must be done!
The Sabbath was made...to restore you,

to be loved by your Lord.

So rest your souls and let the flesh perish for a day
to dwell in Me.

Let go of your daily world.....and come to Mine...
I will revive and restore your souls in the midst of My love.
I Am Yeshua, the Lord of the Sabbath.

For a moment....let My heavenly world come to you.
For a moment...feel My presence in your heart.
For a moment My angels will come to you....
to sing and dance My love songs....
so that you will be able to see the rainbow and its colors.
My covenant only if you don't look back...
don't look down.... rather look above.

Let Me in My love.... open the gates..... for love.

My Sabbath blessings....in your heart will shine.
Only My shalom...and the rainbow in the sky for you to have.

If in your heart My commandments and obedience...
learn in the Sabbath, to wait upon, to fall in love.
Until My kingdom come.... My will be done....
Until the next Sabbath comes....and you
will see the rainbow in the sky.

Stitch by Stitch

Stitch > > by stitch....
I Am the mender of hearts....
> > >
> > Awake! Arise oh Zion....awake My beloved !
The heart has stopped.

> > Awake ...arise My people for I Am in you always.
Come with Me.
> > I see the horizon.... I see to the ends of the
seas.
> > I see your heart ...cannot feel...
choices .... choices.... choices....
broken in pieces you are at the time.
> > >

—————•❧❦•—————

> > {Goy:} Mend my heart oh God....
> > Come and repair the tear.....for it hurts.
> > >

—————•❧❦•—————

> > >
> > Choices...choices.....you have...
stand fast......be still in My name...
the light of My love will repair your brokenness.....at
the time.

> > Your questions I hear.......like a rainbow they go around.

> > >

> > Come back to Me.....I Am...mending your open wounds.

> > As you speak to Me ......I listen.......!!

> > >

————◆◈◆————

> > {Goy:} Father I feel completely lost......and as I do

I feel the death of the darkness ....that surrounds
at the time.

Wait for me my Lord ....I am drowning in fear...
without you I can't go on.
Then I ask you....why the heart has become so sad.....
tears ...tears.
Is it evil that I have become?

> > >

————◆◈◆————

> > >
> > Pride....prideful self......
words....wounds of pride....selfish you are...
surrender to Me.......said the Father.
> Know that I Am your God....great Adonai......
I Am pressing down on you.......for your heart has to
disappear... so to belong to Me.

> > >

55

> > Because I love you with all My heart...
I come to you with situations that may seem to bring
horror to you,
but to Me that I Am holy....it's the door to
salvation......for your own heart......
and the ones about to come to Me.
> > >
> > My child you will stop......you will stop....
for ...I....the Father......see you with great mercy
and love.
> > >
> > I need of you.......to surrender your heart completely.
> > >
> > My plan of salvation is......salvation for all......
for all...for all who will believe in Me.
> > >
> > I will mend your heart......with a lesson for you to
learn of My plan.
> > >
> > I will mend your heart......with love.
> > I will mend your heart.... With trials....
I will mend your heart only.... through My beloved
Son Yeshua, Jesus,
the King of all...
for His heart is whole, perfect in Me,
carrying the word to save all.
> > >
> > For He has the power to save, change & restore
what you do to your own, when you afflict yourself.
Wounded by pride and disobedience.

> > >

> > Disobedience of the heart.... disobedience ...that
I will stop.

> > >

> > For I Am the Father.... the one
who's will you refuse to know...
when pride enters in your heart.

> > >

> > Have I not shown you My loving ways,
for you to know that it is in you?
I come to give salvation to the ones that are broken
with no other choice .... but their own choices.

> > >

> > I Am trying your heart with trials...and trials...
because I love you....and I need of your tender heart
to perform My love and mend the ones with a broken
heart.
I had a heart like yours once.

> > >

> > Remember My beloved...
> > I had a heart like yours once.... broken for sin...
sin that destroys the purity of heart!
It tears the wholeness in you.

> > >

>> Pride and rebellion .... stubbornness ....

your own ways of changing...not giving.... not surrendering.
> > >
>> It is all pride....all come from the dark you allow....

to enter in your heart.

> > Remember that I Am in control > >
> > I will not give you more than what you can carry on
your own...
for I ....know the weight of the cross.
> > >

> > {Goy}>> Father .... I do not want to.

> > Neither did I My child...
> > >

> > My child....the Father's will had to be done, for
the Father is mighty....
His plan will be what it will be.

> > >

> > Shema ....listen.....oh Zion...
do not arise in rebellion & pride, rather, come to Me.
> > I will nurture you ...so that you will perform ...
the great task the Father has upon.
> > >

> > I hear you calling Me," Lord...
Lord mend my broken heart."

> > But pride has entered in you.
> > How can I mend your broken heart .... when you
fight Me?
> > How can I repair the tears...stitch by stitch....
when your pride is between My hand and your
heart...?
> > >
> > Remember what you wrote ...at the time....
"Simpleness Among the Thorns"....
> > >
That is how I will come to you.......and mend
your tears.
when tired and broken, when you trust in Me .
> > >
> > Be simple....be humble....be loving....be
truthful.
> > >
> > Let others see My love light through
you.... even if you do not want to…..
for it is a command to you.....to obey what the Creator
has prepared.
> > >
> > Pride will possess your hearts with
agony....anxiety & sorrows.
> > Pride breaks the spirit and flesh.....if you allow the
enemy to have control…
when you become....your own....and leave the Mender of

hearts behind…and ….
leave My simpleness....to go to the thorns.......thorns
that will tear apart.
> > >
> > Then, then ... My child.... even if you are in pain
I will wait ...wait.... until…
you repent.... until you surrender in simpleness….

> > Ready to allow Me.... to come to
you and mend the broken
heart.
> > >
> > I Am Yeshua, Jesus.... the one
who mends the broken heart.
> > >
> > The one.... who repairs with love....
the one.... the one who sees and feels the tears of
your own heart.
> > >
> > I Am with you....I live in your broken
hearts.
> > I feel.....and with My own tears..... I cry your own.

> > >
> > Yes I will heal you.....in simpleness ....
the same simpleness....that at the time...
when My own flesh was ripped apart…
My own heart was broken....for evil seeks to destroy
a whole heart...a mended heart.
> > >

> > Be in My peace.....My child.....I Am ....mending your
heart.....
stitch by stitch.....stitched with love.....
stitched with kindness....
stitched with grace & mercy.
> > >
> > Stitch by stitch....I Am Yeshua, Jesus, the
Lion of Judah.
Always mending your broken heart.
> > >
> > Be aware of My people.....in need of My touch....
you will see them....you will know them......
for their hearts are broken.....as yours was.
> > >
> > The mender ....I Am....who comes and
stitches....your life's.....
for you to go about with Me on the road.

Ready to be simple...among the thorns......
and bring the broken hearted....
the ones who's tears and wounds...are so deep....
that I will need of you ....to work with Me....
> stitch > by > stitch >...
so that the great .... Father, Abba... will see My own
being healed by your obedience.
> > >
> > Your own wounds ....open My wounds from the
past....
but....every time you go about with Me ....
and stitch > by > stitch

heal others in the name
of His great love...His great law.... My wounds and
yours....

disappear.

> > >

> > His love and mercy will be with you on ....
the road....

> > He will give you.... through Me..... the strength to walk
on the hostile road.

Road that you may not like....in which the comfort of
your heart will be tried.

Then remember.... your own people .... the ones who the
Father chose.

Remember .... the rainbow...the moon ...the
stars.... the creatures

of the air .... land.... seas...

they were all made to perform according to their
Creator...

and they go about.... shinning all.... in one....

for if one misses and fails.... the great plan will
prevail.

> > >

> > Be of a strong heart My little people....
be of courage.

> > Be of My joy....be in Me at all times....

I Am here and there.... I was ...I Am ...I will be.

> > >

> > Open your hearts and show Me the tears.....

then My love will begin the work ...to restore you
again and again....

for I was made to bind... stitch > by > stitch.....your
human heart....
and as your tears are being repaired....that brings
healing to the Kings heart.
> > >
> > And when I hear the door.....and turn around....and
I see you....
with tears of humbleness...and a crown of thorns......
the time of mending begins.... the time of grace
begins...
the time of healing love begins.... (sighs).
So to get you ready for our next journey.... until the day
of My return.

> > The day in which My heart and yours will be whole in
one in the Fathers love.
> > >

> > Until then My beloved.... awake ...arise....
Oh Zion......
come with Me ...the road it is filled with endless
tears and tears....
broken hearts...ready to be mended....
by My holy hand and the simpleness in you among
the thorns.
> > >
> > Until then My love ...stich by stich...
come with Me....for the time is near.
> > >
Until then......until then...

Come with Me.....and do not let pride tear the
mendings of My great love.

> > >

For I, Yeshua‚Jesus.... lives for the mending of
your lives.

> > >

The Wedding Day

The great day.... the day of light...
Oh, Holy Spirit.... messenger of love....
carrying the love of the great King....
to His bride.... love songs from the throne.

For all the lost.... for all the ones seeking the perfect love....
I send to you My message.... My messenger
speaking my love songs to you....
My heart diligently.... seeking through
the day through the night.

Look at Me....I Am the one who was at the cross....
for the day of the cross was the day of
the great wedding between...
your heart and Mine.

The day I gave you My all.... My heart.....
My sacrifice........My love.
On that day, My love did cover ...all
the heavens .... all the stars.
For that day, My love for you was sealed with
my blood......and you my bride covered....
with linens and whites.
For the day of the wedding.... the day of the
cross.... the day I gave you My all.....

Was the day the King bowed down to you at the cross...
human kind.......with eternal love.
For I Am Yeshua ...Jesus...your bridegroom......
and you are My bride.

Wait for My return.... wait in great faith....
for after the great battle…..
after the great judgment day.... I will
come for you....as your savior....
with all My army of angels.
I will come on the time .... where light
and dark will be one....and
only the light of the king will be seen....
The 7 lights...will shine all the heavens....by the
purity of the oil....of your faithful hearts.

I will bring all the heavens to earth.... fire, holy fire will be.
Trumpets announcing the return of the one King....
The king that was hung on the cross.

Dark will surrender to the day of no hour.... the great battle....
but My bride will be surrounded by the ark angels.

My land My beloved Jerusalem will be surrounded by all
the armies of the great Father....dark will perish forever.

Until then .... you My beloved.... wait for
My return ....be prepared....be ready.

Until then.... let your wedding garments....be ready.
Until then.... let your hearts be in
complete purity.... for that is the
aroma that pleases the bridegroom.... your King.

See....the flowers of the valley.... their beauty ...I created.
As I see the beauty of your hearts in purity waiting for Me.

Every time you call upon Me....Yeshua Jesus....
as you deny the flesh…. deny sin....
I will create.... a new flower until the valley it is fulfilled.

Every battle that you win.... in My name......
the heavens rejoice with healing
rains pouring to My land.... with healing
and blessings... and prosperity.

Put on your garments.... dress up with new
flowers......receive My healing rains.
Hear My love songs in your hearts....
Know that.... I Am..... the one who sends you
the Holy Spirit.... the white dove....
bringing messages from the throne.

My covenant with you will be fulfilled....
the Ketubah.... you must read....
You must obey ...you must fulfil.
You must know about the one Creator
of the greatest story of love.
My love is fulfilled in every word....in every scroll…

and you as My bride, you must fulfill your part....
For our hearts to be one.... under the Father's mitzvoth.

Believe in Me.... Yeshua, Jesus.........the everlasting Son.
Do not despair in the times to come......
do not give in unto evil......for I did not give up at the cross.
Do not despair.... for you will witness
the signs of the great end.

Know that ...I Yeshua....your bridegroom......
is with you always.
For I Am the beginning and the end....
For I created the beginning and the end.

Be in peace....be strong!
For a crown of thorns will be exchanged....
for the crown of the bride....
With flowers, I created for that day.

For on the day of the wedding.... it will be the last cup....
the7th day.... for the last time
for the last time....
your name will be announced.... proclaimed....
as you are called upon....
to the presence of the king.
Truly.... truly....
The wedding of your dreams!

A wedding that will never end.... for My love and shalom....
will seal eternal love.
And the love story will be fulfilled....as the heavens rejoice.
For My bride, will come to the kingdom of all the heavens....
With linens and whites.... that signify the purity of heart....
That pleases the heart of the one Creator of all love.

The Waiting

Rest in My peace....I Am calling you....
close your eyes and lean on Me.
Let the cares of the world disappear....I know of your needs.

Can you hear the fierce storm? Great thunder from
storm clouds announcing change... warnings......
by My command.
Great lightning .... showing the path of
the storm.... warnings of love.

Yet...if you are still....and enter in My
peace.... you will be able to feel...
the soothing of heavenly rains......coming
your way to cleanse your heart....
Rain drops with the sounds of love.... like the violin...
Soothing like My love.... for you My beloved people.

How much I desire....to bring My peace and shalom
to you, finding your hearts ready to receive.

Throughout the ages....I had to calm the
great storms.... to calm your hearts.

Had the sun turned into darkness.... as a warning of
what your life's will be ...without the light of the Son.

Had to call the great waters....to destroy....

That in the eyes of great Adonai....
had no life.

Yet....you still pray to the gods that at the time were buried
with you underground not being able to save you!.

Shema.....hear ......My warnings......hear the sounds
of the great heavens.......for I, the great I Am,
call upon them.....
As a warning of love....as a reminder of what was destroyed....
and what it will be destroyed at the end of time.

For....the storm that makes all tremble....and the lightning
that makes you blind.....are a call for what is to come.
Warnings I Am sending you.....as a reminder
of the mighty hand of Great Adonai.

Shema....hear...tremble and change your wicked hearts.
Leave the darkness of the world.....let the
fear of Great Adonai reign in you....
let My love be in you........let My healing
rains perform miracles of the heart.

Truly.....if you are at that time.... in the midst of the
great storm....and you choose to be in Me.....change....
be of a brave heart.......leave the world of
destruction behind ...follow Me....
The healing rains that will come in the midst of the
great storm.... will cleanse your heart and minds....
even in the midst of destruction desperation and agony.

I will protect you My beloved people.

Truly......you will be shadowed by My heavenly archangels......
and only the soothing sounds of My love ...the sound of the
rains you will feel.

For the ones who refuse Me.....and have no
fear of My Father's commands...
Every sound of the great heavenly
thunder........will be heard....

Every strike of the great heavenly
lighting .... will make them blind.

For the light of the Son....will disappear....
and in the dark, they will remain...
cast out forever......to the lands of the desolation....
where they will meet with the gods they lived for.
No hope ...nor grace from the throne.... Selah.

For you ....My beloved people....My brave hearts....
whom I see from the throne....from My heart....
for you who show Me great courage and faithfulness
in the midst of the battle.......the world.
You will be rewarded.....I will call upon ...heavenly
rains....heavenly eternal love....
As a gift from the Spirit......of My Father great Adonai.

For I Am Yeshua ....Jesus...the one
who calls upon the storms....

The one who calls upon the restless seas.....
Calls upon....the light of the sun.....the
light of the moon and the stars....
For the glory of My beloved Father.

--------------------Great Adonai------------------------
Selah

CHAPTER 4

Warnings

Yeshua the Great Angel

I Am Yeshua the great angel.
Have no fear for I Am your shield....
I Am eternal.... alive…. I Am in you.

Fear no men.... the enemy arises.... from dawn to dusk.
Have no fear my child.... I Am your King...
My angels you will see.... arise from the
horizon.......with eagles' wings....
to protect the ones in need of Me.....seeking Me.
Angels wings.... I Am sending to you....
for you to see My Kingdom.
For you to know that ...the great Father....
upon the enemy is.
Waiting for the appointed time......to be destroyed.

Angels....for you to see….
My Kingdom.

My armies are charging in the heavens......
ready to blast the skies....
with trumpets of triumph.... they will seek for My beloved.

By God's wrath......they will destroy the dark....
with no mercy.... until the end of times......
the skies will be broken.... with sounds of war...

Calling My name...for you to know that......
This is the coming that you are waiting for.

My angels you will see.... saving My people
and My beloved Jerushalayim.

My angels will come.......heaven and earth will be one....
the oceans will no longer be....
This earth of Mine will disappear......to the end of times.

It is the cross that will remain as a sign for the wicked...
dark angels.... their heads and wings will be cut off.
No branch of the vine will be safe for
the darkness that is within…..
dark angels......no more.

As a sign of My love......My light is in you....
I Am giving you angels wings.... for you to come to Me.
I Am Yeshua, Jesus….. the giver of angel's wings.

Wings that will allow you to see My
Father's kingdom of peace....
only through Yeshua, Jesus, the Lord of Lords....
The Lord of the great army of heavenly angels.

My wings you will receive...
I Am ...the Great King…. with loving
wings...with iron wings....
with judging wings....

Wings that will write through you....
to tell of My endless love....as you believe and obey....
The almighty Great Adonai.

I Am Yeshua....the great angel.... giving you authority....

to speak in My Name....
With eagle wings...loving wings.

The Watchman of the Bride

Gates of love.....guardians of My place....
watchman of My wall...!
Fire in your hearts.......fire that will last for an eternity
I Am your God ....I Am your mercy and love.....
Close the doors and protect My dwelling Zion......!!

My angels will go....they will take place on
the twelve gates...they will protect the gates of
My beloved dwelling place.....My bride.
Keep the battle.....move on....I see you from above.
Keep praying....keep dwelling....I Am with
you......I Am your Almighty God.
I will protect...I see your face......mercy will come......dew
will cover all.....all under your God......you must go on.

Gates of My heart....watchers of day....
Watchers of the night.....make a covenant with Me....
I will restore.
With your eagles' wings and the angels
of your Lord .... We will destroy.
Fire.... holy fire.....is your Lord.
My fire ....I will send to My beloved dwelling place....
because ....I Am your God ...I Am the
almighty Lord of the covenant of love.
Seven times I will go upon.....seven times I will see....
seven times seven...I will declare ...I will judge.....

My trumpets will sound to the mountains to the sky to
the place where My heart dwells on....Jerushalayim.....
My bride...My love!

Mountains and oceans will cry....for the
Lord you did not cry out for....
For the King you did not see....blood of My
covenant.....holy blood of My own.
The spirit of peace will land....will talk...
will whisper....will seal My love.
My people and My servants will come....
will come to the promised land .

12 iron gates will close.....at the time that will finally come.
I Am holy....I Am your God.....listen...shema!
Open your hearts until I come....
Stay within My 12 gates...stay within the bride.
We will come....
The Lord your holy Father and the King Son... Will come
to mitzva...to dwell and rejoice....in My land in My heart!

Take place ...find your souls .... for your Lord....
take place.... protect...watch day and night.
I Am the light.
Zion will see Me ...I will shine upon your hearts...

Keep fighting …. I see you…I know
you….I Am protecting you
watchman of the wall......dwelling temple….
. I Am .... I Am.

Hear the angels sing My holy name......declare goodness of
your Lord....and the end!

Jerushalayim....Jerushalayim.... hear the angels come.... hear
the angels sing ...I Am your God, the holy one of Israel.

Fire, I Am, written in the tablets.
Fire, I Am, written in your hearts.
Fire, I Am, obey....be the watchman of My dwelling wall....
wait for Me.....wait for My Beloved Son... We will reign and
dwell forever in your heart.
It is My command to watch My beloved land!!!
Zion....will reign.... The kingdom will
prevail....My bride Jerushalayim....
I Am the holy one of the land......
The almighty of Israel.......watch.... watch....
My wall day and night...I Am holding you in
My arms......until the gates are closed.....
~I AM~

Breath . . . . . . I Am Here

As your journey is complete....
Another day that you served Me...
My heart it is pleased....
Breath, I Am here!

My name was called every time.... every
hour through your day....
I saw you ....at times.... gasping for air....
Yet, you called My name.

I Am holding every situation.... with peace...
all you need to do......it is call My name......
that I will breath upon you.
Hashem!

Trough Me ...you are learning to breath....
I Am ...loving your obedience.
As your branches.... sprout.
As your spoken words are all about Me, your King.
it is My peace that allows you to breath.

As fertile as soil is.
As the green pastures and flowers....
as the tress .... abundant....... in branches.
They grow by the grace of My breath......
and My healing rains....
As it is the obedience of your heart.

Pastures surrounded by trees,
I planted them.
So that they will grow tall and strong.
As they receive the light of the Son from above....
so that their branches will grow...to be a
shelter for the ones in need of Me.

I planted them....so that their fullness will look upon....
so that.... their branches will bear.... heavenly fruits....
so that their trunk...will be strong enough....
to support the ones on the road....
gasping for air....in need to lean on....in need of My breath!

My breath will nourish......a living tree.
My love will flourish.... with blessings and leaves.
With a gust of My breath.... flowers from heaven should be.
I planted them.... if fruitful....... I will keep them alive....
When harvest time.... will come.

Forbidden the ones .... whose branches....
and roots are not fulfilled....
forbidden if.... not able to offer a shade
to the ones in need of Me...
unable to bear fruit....
No beauty to glorify My father......The King....
My breath then.... will.... condemn.
My breath ...and fire......ashes underground.... they will be.

As for you .... My breath.... Living is......
as long as with obedience....and discipline from heart....
You call upon Me....you breathe through Me.
The roots are already in you...
My healing rains.... are watering you.

Your growth ....as a living tree....
will be complete.... only through the Son's.... Breathe!
Fulfilled you should be .... to offer.... your fruits and flowers...
to the heavenly Father as an offering of love.

I have all the power....by My breath....
heavens and earth are fulfilled...
yet .... My loving kindness.... sees you growing....
day by day.
As you call My Name......as you gasp for air.
As I breath on you My healing rains.

Deny Yourself to Receive

As you dwell in Me.....My love covets.... your being.
As you strive for Me.....as your heart looks upon Me.
It is your humbleness that leads you to dwell in Me.
As you deny your flesh to come into My holiness.

In times of despair, in times of trouble.... do not give in!
Deny your fear as you receive Me.
Loose yourself in prayer.... your request will be fulfilled.

Purify yourself by denying the flesh…..
as you choose to have eyes that will see.
As you choose to have ears that will hear.
A heart that will deny its own beat…..
and choose to beat along with Mine to be free.

Deny to be bound by the chain of.... hurting words.
Deny yourself of judgment .... from the ones, you love.
Without denying, your spirit will be killed.
This behavior will slave you…..
this behavior will take you to the alleys of destruction.

Inhuman behavior...
that will not allow you to feel My love…
be free and receive.

Obedience to My Father...
as I denied My throne and became flesh....

obedience that took Me to the cross....
to save freedom and love.

Was I not denied again and again?
Because color ....because race
one tear for every denial, My heart blead!

With My open heart My love for you carried every sin.
Your love and denial I took upon...with a crown that
was weaved in My own flesh to set you free.

Denial that took Me to the place where
the temple veil had to be torn.
Denial that took Me to the place where
the rooster called 3 times
as they denied Father,Holy Spirit and Yeshua the Son!

Denied your human flesh to be whole and by doing so....
You are saving and not cursing the ones in need of Me.

Know that there is nothing higher than to please
the Father!!
As you deny yourself to fulfill the great law.

Show your love to others as much as you love Me....
deny yourself to acknowledge Me.
Knowing that above all your needs and desires and dreams
the great love lays in the power to believe.
Learning to deny the flesh will bring you closer to Me
as My love you receive.

Let love be sought to conquer fear.
Let love be the light to conquer the dark.
Let kindness be the channel to conquer anger.
Mildness of heart and purity will set you free and
will allow you to feel My love.

As the almighty Father, from His Holy throne,
rejoices in you as you learn to deny the flesh.
Rejoices in you as your obedience sets you free.
Rejoices as He pours His love into you
as you are able to receive.

Stop living for the flesh, begin dwelling in Me
stop breathing.... begin loving....
not asking.... rather listening...
begin giving....and receive....
Me.

Deny.... What is not right.
Deny....what abolishes My law.

Deny …. what controls bad behavior and hurting words…
that destroys My love.
Deny …. what destroys My heart.

Can you feel My love?
Can you feel Me dwelling in your hearts...?
Can you feel the need to receive My endless love?

What grater love is there than
the denial I took upon the cross in the name of love.

Do Not Take Me With You

Keep on writing.... keep on trusting.... keep on loving.
My love comes to you...My love pours to you.

You will never know when I come to you,
unless you listen to your hearts.

Stop living for the flesh and come to Me.
When I will call you.... when I will come to you...

When would you see My face....
again, and again.... time to time...?

Time, it is an eternity.... My time it is unknown to you.
The time you are waiting for will come
as you listen to your hearts.

Your request, your desires to the Father, all will be fulfilled
If you come to Me.

I Am Yeshua Jesus the one who dwells in the midst
of the mystery of all the heavens and stars.

I Am, Yeshua, Jesus the one who dwells between your
hearts...and the great Almighty One, Adonai.

Come to Me, come to Me.
The beauty of My love it is in the midst of all My creation.

Can't you see, can't you feel what the past has brought to all
humankind?

I Am your King....the one who will intercede on the final day.
The day in which Great Adonai will
declare the beginning of the end.

Do not bring My name when in the midst of your sin,
For I Am holy.

Stop calling My name in the midst of your false gods, for
I Am holy.

As you choose sin you choose to drown
yourself in your own blood....

for My blood was poured out for your
salvation once and for all.

Know that I Am holy …. know that I Am your God....
Do not take Me with you.... when you choose
to walk into the alleys of destruction.

Do not take Me with you when willfully
you are to sin against Me
for I have shown you the dark....
For I have shown you My light...

I have shown you My love ...My power.

I have given you My own beloved Son....
I have given you My all to carry the
weight of your sins on the cross.
I Am giving you the word written in the scrolls.

I have shown you My light, as the dark angel
once was in the light of great Adonai......and
became the dark of the underworld....
became of the serpent destroying the beauty of My creation.

Why do you take My holiness with you into the swamps...?
where the dark, the snake dwells.?

Why do you take My love to places ....
to be tainted and destroyed...?
Did not I come to save you in the name of love...?
Did not I give you My heart for you to
be in eternal love and shalom.

Didn't you see the wonders and the
rainbow given by Great Adonai?
Dark was dark, light He created.

You know of Me, I created you.
I walk with you; I will never leave your side.

Know that I Am holy, I Am your God.
Are you of a pure heart ready to receive Me?
so, that I may walk with you and live in you.

You know of Me I created you,
I gave you the living word for you to be of a pure heart.
For you to receive My peace, My shalom.

My word, the weapon you need
to shield you from the dark angel.
When you will be tempted by the enemy,
when you will be ready to give up all hope,
when you will say yes to sin and die in the hands of the dark...
If you choose
to call My name with adoration....in repentance in love
I will then raise you up in My power.

Know that I Am your God, that you will come in reverence,
in repentance, with your heads covered, knowing that I
Am the God who sees the inner layers of your hearts.
Make clean the inside of the cup.

For if only you cover your heads and cleanse your
hands before Me only on the outside….
Know that I see the darkness inside.

So, I tell you.... nothing has changed from the past.
Before you come to Me....

cover your head and hearts.... cleanse your
hands and hearts from within.

Take off the covering of your feet for
your ground becomes holy.

I Am great Adonai, I Am holy.
I will have no mercy.... I have shown you the love of My light.

I will be looking for repentance ....
you must circumcise your hearts.

I walk with you, I Am with you......I came to save you.
My heart, it is yours .... My love it is yours.

My word it is yours.... My sacrifice it is yours....
know that I Am holy......My beloved Son is living holiness.

Only through His holiness you will have My mercy.
Only through Him mercy will come.

For I Am ...great Adonai the God who forgives.
For I Am the God who judges with no mercy for the wicked.

Know that the one who uses My holy name in vain....
know that .... the one who carries it to sin.....

dead will be.......dead will be!

My beloved Son Yeshua, Jesus .... the King of all love,

The king of My beloved Jerushalayim....will return
to intercede in the name of love.

I will then pour mercy over your heads......

If you repent......if you choose to deny the flesh.

if you learn to disappear when in My
presence.

If you tremble with love when My name it is to be proclaimed
If you learn that I Am your only God, the living God.
The Creator of all living and dead.

CHAPTER 5

Warfare

I Was Made To Save

I was made to save!

I was made to worship You my Lord.

I was made to save but My people would not listen to Me.
I was made to love you, I was made to protect....
I was made and you were made.

I AM in the existence of all.....
I made all the stars.......and the very sand on earth.......

the midnight skies.

The very creation was made to give you
a place surrounded by My love.
By the grace of My Father all became alive....
And I was made to save.

and I was made to worship You my Lord.

My people .... they cry out to Me. They deny Me.....
I see their eyes close.... when by their life's ...I pass by.
Even if they see the smallest of the birds,
their colors, their love songs.
Even if they see the great creatures of
the seas, the great mountains.
The moon that gives you light by night, the
sun that gives you light by day...
My people would not believe in Me.
So I was made to save.

My Lord I was made to worship you.

You My child were made to perfection.....
but sin came upon all human kind.
And you My child became of a weak
heart.....so I was made to protect.
You know of good and evil.....you also know of Me....
but you rather close your eyes when I Am by you
passing by, with My hands open wide.....
you rather walk into the dark.
So I was made to save .....the Father's plan of love......
I Am your Savior.

I came to you....to be among you.
Witness the miracles of great Adonai.

I was made the word....for you to know the journey of love.
As you read the word, wrap around in
your tallit that becomes a shield.
I became a child like you.....I became a man like you....
and on the cross ...I was made to save all humankind
die in the flesh.... for you to live in Me.
But My people would not listen.....would not see love
and obedience that comes from the throne.

I was made the Sabbath day.....for you to come to Me.....
rest in Me..... day I have prepared for you and Me.....
To take you to the places unknown....
to restore a place of shalom.
But My people would not listen.

I was made to save you from the place.... that I would
not return until the very end.... the last day.
A place the Father had to create....place with no
hope...no escape....no mercy ...no light....no life.....
no air to survive.....were lifeless creatures dwelling
in sin.....and the angels of darkness.
A place where My people will go.

My heart mourns for you.......for I see
your steps walking to that place.
Your eyes only looking at what shines....promises of
the dark.....that at the end will become ashes.
You live to fulfill the flesh with sin.....
holding on to the gods made of stone.

None of your gods were made to love and save.....
they were made to destroy for they are the gods.....
of the place ....I call hell.

My land ...My beloved Jerushalayim....
the place where I was made to save...
attacked by the angels of dark.....a place of miracles.....
place of love......the place chosen by the Father to be
The center of the greatest story of love......
story between human and holy.

The story that is hated and hunted by the angels
of dark......for they know that at the end....
I will return....I will return.
Day in which I will see and seek.....the human heart
resting in My peace.......where they will remain!
Day in which I will see and seek the human heart troubled
by sin.....judgement they will see.......and remain!

Until then.....My beloved.....if you choose
to be saved......I will save you...
I will.
Know that I never rest.... nor by the midnight
skies...nor by the sun light....
Always waiting for you to say.... My Name....
and ask Me to come into your life.
Give Me your all.... not part of you.
I will restore your life.... you will open
your eyes.... and finally see....

the smallest of the creatures.....the mighty
mountains.....all what is living, surrounding you.
All worshiping your Creator....along with you....you
the piece missing in this, the great story of love.

I Am.....Yeshua.....Jesus.....I was made to save.....
And you and I.....were made to worship.....
the Father...the great ... I AM.

I AM the Father's Lion...
I AM the Father's Lamb

I Am the Father's Lion ....I Am the Father's Lamb.
The battle it is upon....the great day of forgiveness.....
the day of repentance........the days of awe.....!!
Hear the sounds of the battle.....here the sounds of
your heart beating along with the battle drums...
beating along with My heart.
Hear the Lion roar....to the people on earth....
for the Great One comes with sounds of glory.

Hear My roaring awaking you from the dead.
Great heavenly armies....angels and archangels all.....waiting
for the great command....the hand of the most Holy One.
The heavens will roar....the oceans will be silent.....
the moon and the stars will shine one more time.
Great winds you will see...not knowing where
they come from or where they go.
But in the midst the Lion will be....and the only
light you will see.... Will be of the Son.
As I come back to you.... prepare your
souls for the great day, it is upon.
Repent....forgive....
surrender your heart as the Lamb....
do not give up.......the battle, it is Mine.
All I need is you....your heart needs to
return to the heavenly camp....

where you will a line with the great armies .....I need you
to seek the lost....the ones who are being destroyed by
My enemy...your enemy .....the angel of dark.

Do not be afraid.....be strong in Me....and as I did.....turn
to the ground the tables of the merchants who collect
your souls along with silver and gold.
Open the gates of the cages of the ones who remain in the
dark....as I did set them free.....and proclaimed My holy name.
I Am with you ... Hear the Lion roar.....I will give you
the strength to conquer and roar in the enemies camp.

My power it is in you...say no to what
destroys.....and eats you alive!
Learn to forgive your own.....forgive others
with compassion as the Lamb.
As the Lamb who forgave....the ones who turn My Father's
temple into a den of thieves.....caged the oppressed.

For the Lion and the Lamb are of one heart.
The great will of My Father had to be
done....it will be done again.
For I was made to obey...with My own life....
made to forgive in love and kindness.
I Am the Father's Lion ....I Am the Fathers Lamb.

To repent it is your battle....My wisdom is
given if you ask....grasp it ...do not let go.
Repent....do not return. Walk....do not
stop.....commit to the great battle.

Never go back ...never return from the
place where I Am saving you from.

Be in silence ....away from the world....hear the
beat of your own heart......I Am there.
The king roars to the great heavens ....
with great sadness....sorrows...
when I see that you doubt Me......when the dark comes to
you and I see you walking back....to the enemies camp.
The heavens then cry.....here My roaring, the
oceans, the moon and the stars they all tremble!
For the King is losing one heart.

I die for you.....I live in you....I Am with you.....I Am
giving you My power to repent.....return to Me.
Hear My roar ...the Lion never rests ....never rests ....
going about the enemies camp... opening cages....
setting you free.... the door it is already open!.

Forgive the ones who have chained your life.
Love them as they are.... save their hearts....
for they choose not to hear the roaring of the Lion.
They denied the tenderness of the Lamb.

Come with Me.... to the battle field.....
roar with Me ....for righteousness.....justice.....
roar with Me....for the purity of the heart.....roar for freedom!.

Roar with Me against the enemy when he is
about to take the one next to you...as a prey.

See the one next to you ....not as your enemy.....
but as a prey that has been attacked.
Do not judge or condemn....love with a
heart of a Lamb.....forgive....repent.

I will roar My judgement....great judgement.....on the
day .....for the ones who choose to remain inside the cage.
The ones who go about with the angel of dark
and attack the already oppressed....
knowingly ....by choice.....they choose to remain
in the hunt of My people.......My land......
My beloved Jerushalayim.....great armies will come.....
the days of awe...the day of Great Adonai Tzevaot.

So I Am using these hands to roar....for I will never
rest until you come back to the heart of the Lamb.

I did roar…..on the day of the cross.....
I will roar on the day of awe......I Am roaring on
the days of atonement....the days of teshuva.

As the Lamb was sacrificed in the name of pure love....
the name of forgiveness.....the name of peace.

Sacrifice for all human kind.
Slain...blood covering that purifies all sin....
blood that seals the repented heart.
Blood that conceals the truth.... the seal of My love for you.

Let My roaring awake your heart.... let
My blood restore your life.
I Am the roaring Lion ....the King with a heart of a Lamb.

I Am the one .... Jesus....Yeshua...!
I AM the Father's Lion .... I AM the Father's Lamb.

Not of This World

Not of this world .... I want to be....
My heart belongs to you my Lord......
Take me to the places unknown, where
I dwell in You....Oh King.

Not of this world .... I want to be....

This world .... My beloved.... comes and goes.
This world does not stop.... destruction
and salvation will come....
they forgot about.... the living God....Great Adonai.
They worship to what destruction will bring upon.

My signs are to come....
through the heavens, earth...skies.... will come...
for you to know that ...

I Am ...your God, the Almighty One.

I created you....I gave you this world....
a place to rejoice......not to be destroyed.
But sin has taken upon your daily life's....
your daily bread......daily eyes.

Your hearts…. I see.... only look upon .... of what it is not

108

of the world that I created for you.

You now belong to the underworld....
where destruction is upon....as a sign for the dark....
for... I... your God....sees it all from above.
I see your hearts living a dying life.

Of this world, you choose to become, still I Am your Father.
I Am yours......My love for you, it is eternal.
As a sign, it is the world I created for you.

I great Adonai gave you a land......
fulfilled with My signs of love....
I great Adonai gave you My people...through the scrolls....
I great Adonai gave you all My riches....
for you to know the power and extent of My love.

I gave you this world for you to walk the land with Me....
to dwell in Me... love never felt before....to be in Me.

A part of Me was sent to you, with hope.
A part of My life was sent to you.
My whole was sent to you, from My throne.
With a plan of salvation for you My love...
for I, great Adonai, have cried for
the times I had to destroy My own creation.

Love never felt before was send from Me, My son, Yeshua...!!!
For nothing greater you will ever see....and feel.

My beloved a part of Me came to you....
To tell you of My great love.

My own.... I did send......to My beloved land.
The land I gave you.... for it was tainted with blood.
He came to you....to live ...to love.... to bring life....
to fulfill the law.... you buried in your hearts.

I Am sending you signs of love to bring you to life.
To the world, I created,
a world that is not of your underworld.

Sin destroys the beauty of My love.......
The beauty of the law is destroyed by
the dark you allow in you.

For you My beloved whom I love .... My law is written in you.
The beauty of the land given with honey, milk &Shalom.

For the ones who choose the underworld....
a land of honey and milk will be replaced
with fire and blood…. eternal death.

The greatest sign of My love ...came once to live with you.
Was not He denied.... was not He
ignored.... was not He doubted....
why was not He in your hearts?
For your hearts were and are fulfilled with unbelief.
For you saw My wonders and signs....and you chose sin.

The one I did send....to you.... still with
you is........My beloved Son.
Living truth in holiness....truth in obedience to the Father....
Truth of My power......truth of My law......truth of all love.
The great truth of My own heart...
Had to be crucified......of this world......for you to be alive.

Through you.... I cry....for I see....the lost of this world.

Be of the world ...I created you for.
Be of the riches of heaven.!
Be of My world....be in Me.....be in Me.

I Am great Adonai.
My being, you will never be able to understand.
The mysteries of all heavens and earth.... you will not.
But My eternal love is poured through
My Beloved Son Yeshua.
Love that will heal.... redeem.... save ...condemn.
Love that never ceases to follow you.... wherever you go...
protecting you.... covering you.... waiting for you....
to belong to the world that I created for you.

My compassionate love.... are the signs you see in the world.
Turn to Me I will be there at the time that will finally come.

With great mercy......I great Adonai....I will.... I will....
wait upon you.... if you choose to see
My signs of love...and repent.

Come to My love....and completely surrender in obedience.
I will .... I will.... transform your dying life's...to living!!

Come to Me.....come to Me My child.
The end will come.... the door will
close.....the great end is near.

Dark will remain in the dark.... forever an eternity.
Light will remain in the light.... forever living life.
They will never meet again!

For you who's hearts ...I see...following
Me.....in the battle field....
refusing to belong of this underworld....
I Great Adonai......see you with great peace.

I Am blessing your obedience.... from the throne!!

Be strong ...don't give in.
Go about with no fear.... for I Am ...who...I Am ....
your great shield.

Bring My people to Me....waiting ...I
Am ...until the last will come....
will be safe.... will see the King and come to Me.

My beloved Son ...Yeshua, Jesus... will
come to you one last time.

The King's Son .... of all heavens and
earth.... will come ...for you...
who chose to be of the world I created for.

Great armies of angels will come....to announce the King....
you finally will come to Me....for I
have prepared a great feast.
Until the time.... My eternal shalom is in you .... My child.

Until then....on the Sabbath....come to Me.....
I will fulfill you with My word.......My knowledge....
My peace for you to know.....
The great Sabbath it is a command!
The great Sabbath it is the time.... I leave My throne...
to come to you.
I come to you.... through the heart of My Beloved Son,
Yeshua Sar Shalom.
For only through Him ...you will know the Fathers great love.

For He is the King who conquered the underworld......
For He is the king of the world I created for....

He is Yeshua, Jesus, the King of the land
fulfilled with honey ... milk
And eternal shalom!

To The Warrior

To the warrior in the battlefield

I know of you.... your heart I see in the midst of the
battle.
I feel your heart beat arise on the enemy's camp....
I know of you ...your fear.... I also know of your great
courage.

I know the enemy.... you are trying to destroy.... he
dwells in the dark.
As he comes from the underworld
from where he was cast off...
And he comes to your world to attack .... with great hate...
....to destroy what is alive......
your heart, your hope, your joy!

You were trained to perform a task
of honor to defend freedom
and love.
I know the price is high.... for your own freedom is
lost to save another soul.

There is no time .... there is no time....
through the day and through the night......only the warrior's
task that must be done.

The enemy will not cease to destroy.... for the evil one is

the one who reigns their hearts....
they allow evil to come to their hearts...poison their life's
destruction.... desolation.... torture...abuse...
evil only thirsty for darkness....to perform his own
tasks.

So, evil meets good.......good and you My warriors facing the
enemy hiding behind another heart like yours....
a heart that once was free like yours....in peace like
yours.
Until evil came to destroy........for he is against
Me, the only King.
He uses My creation to destroy.

Know My warrior that all My creation was given
a heart.
A heart and mind to make a choice between evil and
good.
And it is My hand.... I will stretch out ...to bring life...
or to bring death.... upon your heart.

Until then ....be strong....be of a strong heart.... be of
a mighty heart.......I Am with you.
Know that I came to this world and left My throne in
obedience to My Father to be a soldier like you....
to protect freedom and love like you.

I did face the enemy every day like you.... hissing
hiding behind another heart....
like a wolf hiding behind a sheep.... for he is

a liar from the beginning
so, he uses the ones who believe in his promises that
ashes will be.
For his heart was removed by the hand of My Father,
Great Adonai.

I Yeshua, Jesus did conquer the underworld .... he knows of
Me....he knows of you....
he knows of My great power.....he knows that I Am the
Lord of the Battle.
He knows of the armies of the great heavens.... My angels,
Arc angels.

The time is coming .... where evil will rise against
evil...it will bring destruction.... on earth.

The time.... is coming where you will witness the heavens....
come to you...with sounds of the battle.
The angels of the King....will come with no mercy to
destroy.... the enemy and the ones who believe in him.

Until then, My warrior, My soldier on earth......stay
strong.......on the battle field.
Know of Me.....the Lord of the battle.
Call upon My Name ...with respect...do not use My name in
vain.
Do not use My Fathers Great Name
in vain...for He is holy and
He is your creator.
The one who will stretch out His hand and will bring....

life or death.

If you do call upon My Name ...and join the spiritual
battle field...
truly, I will send My angels to you in the midst of the
battle to protect.
They will warn you...they will be a shield to you......you
will see them coming.

Know of the Lion of Judah....the people of the Lord
kings and kingdoms .... battles never
Lost.
1 to a 1000....yet they won....by the Mighty Hand of the
Lord of the battle.

The battle is upon...I will be with you.... call My Name
with reverence.... I will bring My armies to you.

I Am a warrior.... I Am a soldier.... I Am a shield to you...
I Am a double sword...to you.
I Am the one who conquered death and
the grave to give you eternal
life.

Know about Me and My battles.... the word was given to
you.
My heart beats along with yours and sounds of
drums in your heart.... believe in Me.....
I Am with you on the battle field.
My armies and the Lion of Judah ...never rest ...through the

day and through the night....
always in the battle field...trying to save one more ...
one more......hear My roar!

I Am ...Jesus ...Yeshua......the one who's mission was ...to
save and to love ....to save your hearts.
To walk with you ....to teach you about the kingdom you are
about to see.
To give you courage...faith....to make you strong.
My price was to be hung on the cross........for
freedom and love. Obedience to My Father.
I Am... your angel......My wings are yours.... I will refresh
your tired souls with eternal peace and love.
I Am the heart beat...... beating along with yours ...in the
midst of the camp.
So, hear the drums of war...hear the heart beat in your heart.
Hear the Lion and the angels roar.

In the Midst of the Battle

The battle it is upon....
I Am your God....I Am....giving you....
eagle wings.... angel wings.
Rise above....to where the rainbow belongs....
where your heart belongs.......with Me.

Wings that will take you to places unknown to you.
Where ...I Am ...waiting for you.

I feel your heart beating along with Mine....
in the midst of the battle ...I Am.....
in the midst of the encampment.... I Am.....
in the midst of the great rainbow ...I Am.

Spread out your wings....... My beloved.
Do not be afraid.... For My army of
angels have the power of all the
heavens...
just follow Me..... through the midst....
for ....I Am....Yeshua., Jesus
The lord of the battle......
The Lord of all.... Jew and Gentile......
the one new man.

A heart to love.... a shield to protect....
wings to rise up .... high above.... are
given to you.... who obey.

I see your hearts destroyed......for they choose fallen gods....!!
Fallen angels.... that in sorrow dwell...
in a battle already lost....
with broken wings.... burning wings.... in
their own flames.... destroyed.
Pride....disobedience and false power.......against....
Yeshua, Jesus the Lord of the battle.... against.... the great
King of Kings!

For you...your obedience .... will raise you
up above with eagle wings....
for I see your hearts.... fighting in the middle of the battle.
Proclaiming My name in holiness.......Yeshua, Jesus .....!!
I see your hearts in the midst of the battle dancing
before the glory.... of the One above all.
Great Adonai eternal.

The battle it is upon.... hear My heart…..
if My angels are sent to you....
and you choose not to obey....
if My shield is given to you.... and you choose not use it ....
if a heart is given to you....and you choose
not to beat along with Mine.
Your wings will be cut off.... until you choose to...
in the middle of the battle, dance for
My heart....to beat with yours!

My covenant of love I will keep....
as I see you with My great army.... every time...... fighting...
one on one.... holy and human ....
in the great midst.... the great battle....my shield covets you.
The flames you won't feel.... the great rainbow you will see...!!

My eternal love....... in the middle of the battle.... will dwell...
will raise you up above ...with eagle wings...!! Angel wings...!!

CHAPTER 6

His Expectations - Gavah

His Expectations

My Lord began by asking me, to use the next words in Hebrew....

Gavah: Expectation.......look upon....
wait.... bind together.... tarry....

Lev: Heart.... seat of mind
and emotions

Shamar: Obedience....to keep.... (sheepfold ...the
shepherd gathering thorn bushes to make a corral to
protect)

Shamar: obedience and Torah.......Torah it is
law ...comes from the word (yarah) the flow
of an arrow or throw something.

Set of instructions
from the Father to the children to teach obedience against
defiance and disrespect.

Kavod: Honor, battle... removal of fear, glory.

Psalm 3.3 ....
Kavod of God....parallel with his bow.

Psalm 28.8 ...who it is:
the King of Kavod....YHVH...strong and mighty.

Kavod: Battle armament, root of Kavod ...heavy.
Ka-lah: completion.
------------------------------Gavah------------------------------
My beloved....... I Am the one who ordains the feelings
in your human heart lev.

Great tenderness......overwhelmed by My love you feel....
Write and write.... words that I design by using
your hands and your heart....lev.

What do you expect from Me......why do you ask
Me.....You pray to My Father in My name.

Your desires ...your needs I see....I Am the God who lives
in you ....I know of your fears.

So I speak to you My beloved people.....My miracles and
your desires are divine and appointed ...
that will be fulfilled through the law written in
the sacred scrolls.

The journey that I have prepared for you has
what you call expectations.....Gavah.
Expectations to live in Me ....so that I will dwell in you.

I Am Yeshua ...Jesus...the law...the Torah......written in you.

I Am ...love, Ahava..... written in you.....lev.
What do I expect? Gavah.....from you My beloved people.
You have all My power to fulfill what lays in the scrolls.
My love should be sufficient to lead you to obedience.
Shamar: .....Obedience that the great Father expects from you.

Obedience that the great Father expected from Me....to fulfill His great command.
To come to you as a human....in obedience....in humbleness....in surrender....
for you to see....hear...touch.....witness miracles of Great Adonai.

The great expectation ....Gavah ....that was fulfilled at the cross.
For every nail...every thorn.....every lash.....was expected to show you of My great love.

Know of what it is to be fulfilled .
All appointed times....
come from My Father who gracefully watches over you with the great hope that you My child....
will finally turnaround from your wicked ways.
Finally be free to witness miracles in your own life.

Great expectations from the Father.....and the Son.

Shamar.....obedience ...Shamar......!! That will lead you to have great courage and be strong.....as I Am.

Know what the dark angel has for you....he will never cease to tempt you to fail, to tempt you.....against Me....!!
But also know that is written in you ....a heart…
Lev.....that will never cease to obey and abide in Me ....if that is your choice.

Kavod...battle!!..... Be of a great heart ...against him......for... I Yeshua, Jesus, I Am your sword.

My expectations …. Gavah .... for you to surrender to great power of your only God.... The great....
I Am.

The father has the power to end it all......at the appointed time.
He expects from you a change of heart....Lev....to the very last breath.....to the last day.
Cry out for forgiveness....cry out for mercy.....change....call on Me....
I will come to you.
But if you refuse to obey till the last day...the last breath....My judgment will come upon.

Shamar: Obey and expect.....expect then a
miracle....expect grace.....
expect the desires to be fulfilled....if you ask.....and pray
as I did.
Abba....let My desires be yours.....let My expectations be
yours ....and not Mine...oh loving Father.

Know My child....That I did perform .... what
was expected from Me to the last breath the last day.

Also know.... if you expect.... and pray for your own
desires and your own will.... failure will be.

Desolation....confusion......distress ...depression....
over and over.... that will lead you to the hands
of the one who was removed from the throne because his
disobedience and seeks to destroy My
Father's creation.
Know of him .... he has rebelled.... cast out to the dark
forever no mercy will ever be.... only the great
wrath......for him and the ones who refuse Me.

Kavod!!! The battle it is upon......what
is expected from you is.... to pick up your
Torah…. Law .... train with it....
be thirsty for righteousness ...be part of My great army
....the army of the King....Great Adonai.
The battle Kavod .... never ends.... while you sleep
.... while you are awake.....I Am.

My angels and I, the Lion, from the great tribe of
Judah....are about to protect.... your human heart.

So....awake ...arise from the dead........know of My
expectations......I Am giving you the power to destroy your....
wicked heart......
and come to the battle, Kavod.
I expect from you.... your whole heart.... whole mind....lev.
I expect from you.... total devotion....
total commitment....Selah.
Clean heart....clean mind....so that the words
that you speak....will be of wisdom......
and not dirt-and dust.....for dust will go back
to dust ......and wisdom will be exalted.....Shamar
obedience.

Expectations that will lead you to ...triumph.
The same victory that I had the day of the great
battle.....the day of the cross.
The day that earth trembled....the day that the heavens
parted to welcome the King Son....
In glory.....in power.....so that My spirit will
remain....in you My beloved people.

Give Me your expectations....in righteousness....
I have the power to fulfill it all.

You have My power .... but it is buried under your sin.
You have My love but it is darkened
by the stiffness of your heart.

.... Lev ....
You have all the riches of the heavens ....
that you try to fulfill....
with the riches of earth.... silver and gold... silver and
gold that I Am expecting you ......to destroy...
Along with the wooden gods you bow down to.

Rather drown yourself....in My word......instruction of love.
Torah!! .... For it is made to save the great love of
Mine.
You My beloved people.

Hear the battle...Kavod!!.... hear the
sound of My love.

Then My child........if you choose for....
your expectations....to be Mine...
your desires.... to be Mine....
your thoughts.... to be Mine....

Your eyes will see.....through Mine.....you will witness
miracles of Great Adonai.
Your ears will learn to hear.....the sound
of My power.....the sound of the
battle.....Kavod.
Breath through My command.

Most of all ....My beloved.....
Your heart lev.....will learn to beat along with

Mine......My blood will be your shield..... My
word will be your sword.

The appointed time will come...and your expectations-Gavah
Will be in completion, Ka-lah'.
All fulfilled....by My love, Ahava.

Your prayers.... your heart, lev ......in obedience.
In obedience Shamar...for the battle-Kavod....
It's calling you ...and it is upon.

Gavah ...Ahava....
.... Lev.....Shamar......Kavod......Ka-lah......

A Change of Heart

Hear My call....a change of heart....
I Am....giving you all My love.

I gave you all you need....to live with peace....and eternal joy!!
Heavens and earth.... fulfill....
your heart and Mine in one.

I see your eyes...looking around.... trying
to find peace and comfort....
where there is none, false idols, and gods!!
At the end of your day.... the end of your journey....
an empty heart.... blind eyes.... not
knowing why, what used to shine...
turn only into dark...and sorrow,
emptiness and sadness left.

A change of heart.... I seek.....My child....
Come to Me and repent.... from your heart to Mine.
A change of heart that will allow you to realize.... that....
I Am....your Creator....your King.

My commandments.... a gift for you to live with peace.
All you need to be fulfilled...was given to you.
My heart living in yours.... till sin was chosen.
A mind to understand the beauty and
grace of My creation and love.

My law was given....to you...to protect you from
the angels of dark and your own flesh.

My power and mystery you can't
understand ....so I gave you a heart.
I Am... The creator of light and dark....
I Am .... The creator of day and night....
I Am ...The creator of heavens and earth....
I created you with one breath....to fulfill My love.

I have nurtured you all the way along....
showing you My walk while in this
earth.... through the scrolls....
giving you My hand.......giving you My heart.......at the cross.
But your heart chose not to see.
Instead chooses what falsely shines...
Making you a slave of the flesh....and the angels of darkness.
Slavery that will kill your spirit.

Repent and call on Me to change your
heart My beloved child...
for My endless love is waiting for you....
to call upon Me.
Waiting for your new eyes to see the only light that will
shine in your life for an eternity.... because this light
comes from the majesty and the mystery of Hashem.
The King above all.... your only God.

To change your heart.... the roots of disgrace must be cut off
so, they will never grow again.

The strength in I Am, your God, will
be given to you if you call upon
My Name... as long as in your heart there is only place
for obedience in My commands.

I Am your King ...you are My beloved children.
My holiness cannot be mixed with your humanness.
My heart cannot beat for you.... if pride.
My heart cannot beat for you …. if hate.
My heart cannot beat for you.... if chaos reigns in you.
My heart cannot beat for you...if your words are to hurt.
My heart can't beat for yours if.... you choose other gods...!

My heart can't beat for yours if.…. My holy
name is cursed again and again.
Most of all My heart dies when your disobedience
makes you blind and by doing so you deny My love.
You deny the one above all....
Your loving Father....Great Adonai.

A change of heart will allow your
heart and Mine......to be one.
A change of heart that will be replaced
with...strength and love.
A change of heart that will see the dark replaced by My light,
joy and shalom.

A heart that will be a shield for the ones in more need of Me.
A heart that will teach others the love
of the great King and the Son.

A heart that will become another angel of My heavenly
army ready to defeat the dark and save others.
A heart that will beat for a righteous life.
A heart that will beat for My law.
A change of heart that will restore your life's
before the great day comes, the harvest time....and only good
fruit from earth will be gathered by My army of angels.
And the fruitless, will be left on the ground....
with no mercy.... to perish forever!
A change of heart that will allow your heart and Mine
to dwell forever and be one.
To please the one above all.... the Great I Am.

Walk My Walk . . . .

I Am the light of the world....
I Am the light of your life
As you walk My walk.
To see the light... you must resist the dark.
As I did....so to save your heart.

For you to know the dimension of My love...
the same walk you must walk.
The veil covering your eyes.... keeps you from seeing.
By seeking My foot prints....as I walked....
your daily struggle.... your heart and Mine will see the light.

As My light ...becomes your new eyes....
My peace and shalom will shine upon your path.
The darkness of wrong doing....... will be replaced....
with the light of a new life.

By choice ...your walk will be from dark to light.

I Am the glory......that with obedience and love...
pleased the Almighty Father.

I Am the glory that conquered the underworld....
I Am the glory that sees your foot prints.... from above.
I Am the glory.... that already has walked your own world.
I Am the glory...waiting for you to seek Me.

I Am the glory.....that through Me your holiness will be.
I Am the glory that has a path for you...... prepared from Me.

You are My glory....walk My walk.
May your walk shine upon others…..
that they may see in your heart......
the passion to conquer the dark.
That they may see in you...... foot prints ....following Me.
That they may see in you......the living light.
I Am the living light.....that will allow
you to..... walk My walk.
I Am..... Yeshua Jesus ...the living light.
The living light that will allow you to see
the Living God!

Face to Face

Ignore and denial, it is a choice we face
every minute of our lives.
Ignoring your great love My Lord….
is ignoring our freedom from the mark.
Ignore and denial…. the walk to death.
By ignoring Your great love, we choose
to be face to face with the
destroyer of humankind.
Most of all great sorrows will come...when ignoring
Your call as You come to us to meet us face to face…
with Your arms wide open and we turn our backs to you.
The one who comes with simpleness of heart.
Heart fulfilled with hope mercy and love.
The past will be brought by denial…. as we choose
to ignore You we'll bring to You tears of
blood, tears of sadness that nail You to the cross again
and our NO's will become the slashes that
will open your wounds my Lord.
So, I cry out to You for forgiveness...give us
another chance to see You face to face.

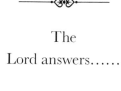

The
Lord answers……

Meet with Me face to face…walk with Me….
be with Me…. come to the unknown….
Receive My love for I, Yeshua, Jesus
was made to save and love.
Your world is spinning out of control…...
lost souls in the midst of a great fog….
fog not allowing you to see Me… face to face.
Great warnings you will see…. you know of
your creator... His hand is mighty.
His heart… it is also all love for you...
love that will save or condemn.
For He is the Great Creator …The Father,
Great Adonai, Tsebaoth, Lord of Hosts.
You choose to ignore My call…. My hand that will save….
My law that will give you the secrets of true
freedom, love and eternal shalom.
Rather you chose to be face to face
with the destroyer of life….
the one who takes a form that you will feel
for…. the shape of lies and darkness….
the shape of the mark…. mark you are taking
for the day of your great sorrows.
And so, I Am sending you great warnings
as it was written in the past.
Denial was their mark…. pride was their
mark …. mark that took them to a place of
no love, nor hope …a place where My light will never shine.
Mark that took them away from Me, to the
great day of sorrow and not joy.

Deny Me not....do not ignore My call ...I
was made to save and love.
I come to you with the great hope that you will
finally choose to be face to face with
Me.
Do not fear to change and trust in the unknown
and leave behind silver and gold.
My heart fades when I, Yeshua, Jesus your King ...come
so close to you so that you ...can feel My breath...
the beat of My heart ...with whispers of wisdom as how to live
your life until My return, and your face turns away from Me.
So .... I, Yeshua, Jesus waits for you in
love...for you.... for you....
so, that you may see My face and the
inner layers of My heart....
Know that ...I was...I Am ...I will be
the same to the end of time.
I will never deny you another chance.
I will never ignore your call.... I will
never stop watching over you.
Be brave and turn your back to the
past.... turn your face toward
I AM.

Pray and pray.... with humbleness ...I
will cleanse your heart...
I will baptize you and circumcise your
heart...in the name of love.
In the Name of the Father, Holy Spirit, and Yeshua the Son.

Face to face, tell Me about your heart....
you only need to come to Me.
For I Am the only way to the Father and the
only way to find forgiveness in love.
For on the day of the cross ...I did receive
you with great love....and denied not.
My angels are all with Me as the Father commands
to protect the ones who are willing
to walk through the narrow gate....and see Me face to face.
The great day of joy.... the day of great sorrow.
Until then ...I live waiting for you to say Selah.
Until then ...I will follow you from afar....as your day goes on.
Until then... I will be with you as you close your
eyes at night and tears of sadness come....
for your heart and Mine cries out when
true love is denied and ignored.
Until then .... I was ...I Am ...I will
be.... Yeshua the King Son....
Until then My heart hopes ...My love hopes....
for the day of great joy....
when finally, you will choose to see Me .... Face to Face ....
And we will meet in the inner layers of My Heart.

Truth... Love... Hope

Hope comes from true love.......the truth you are longing for.
Truth that comes from Me your king.
Your hope is within Me...
Your devotion to Me.... will bring you peace.
Let your heart rejoice.... I Am Yeshua....Jesus.... your true love.

Let the world go around.... let My true love sing to you....
My word is fulfilled with the hope that brings true love.

My true love.... can hear you cry.
My true love.... sees beyond your eyes.
My true love .... knows of your battles.
My true love comes and soothes your heart....
with a dust of hopes...truth ....and joy.

Your eyes are finally open.... yours
eyes can see.... My true love.
Your hopes.... your heart.... are all Mine.
Let your world go around.... stop.... set your eyes on Me.

Now the light it is yours......your hope and faithfulness....
will take you to the place where your eyes are able
through My heart... see!!

I Am your true love.... My child.
I Am yours.... for you are the one who chose to obey....
believe ...hope for ...and see.

I Am the truth...that through your hopes ...love.
Love that ...you are able to feel and live....
when obedience becomes a love song.
When obedience becomes Me.....Yeshua, Jesus, your king.

True love it is only able to shine....
through your eyes.... if you let
the world go around......and choose Me.

Remember....
Your Father is in heaven.... on His
throne watching you grow....
growth .... that will transform your love.
Love that can only be transformed through the truth that
brings Me to your heart........hope that is love.
Love only felt.... through the King Son.

I Am Jesus, Yeshua the Son.
I Am your true love ......that reigns in your heart....
When you let your world go around.

CHAPTER 7

Rest

I Am the God Who Sees

El Roi

I Am the God who sees.... My child....
I see your hearts.... I see your tears....
I see your needs.... I feel as you cry.

I see you daily walk.... I see your steps following Me....
I see your steps away from Me.

The light of My eyes shine.... when you obey the great law.
The true light I Am..., Yeshua Jesus the king Son.
My light feeds your eyes.... for you to follow Me.

My eyes cry out .... when I see you choosing the dark.

My eyes cry out.... when you deny My love by choosing
what is not right.
I see your eyes.... closed.... taken by the dark.
The light is gone....and ....in the darkness you belong.
You choose the dark...rather than My light.

The eyes of your Creator.... tears of Great
Adonai cover all the heavens...all the stars...one more time....
for I created you to be in the light and
safety of My eternal love.

Receive My light in your life.... I Am Yeshua, Jesus,
the King who's eyes sees your human hearts.

My eyes are the light in your life.... My child.
The light of My love will only give you
peace that restores.
Strength to keep your eyes on Me.
The trust you need ...to see.... that My eyes are following you.
Watching over you.... with tenderness ....and endless love.

As I once was feed through the eyes of love from the
Father to endure the great pain......the great sorrow.

The tears I bore at the cross.... I bore for every whip....
for every sin....
but My human eyes did remain on His great light.
For obedience was.... the great commandment I did obey
in reverence to My Father....
The one Creator who's eyes......were merciful to Me.
As My own eyes are with you My child for My love it is
indeed the light that will feed you......with eternal shalom.

I Am the God who sees My child....
I Am the God who blesses your eyes....
if you choose to see Me.

My eyes never rest.... through the day.... and night......
watching over you.... I Am.
My eyes never rest.... for they are
light.... holy .... without flesh.

Through the light of My eyes ...you will see...
all my promises will be fulfilled... all will be....
as it is the promises of My law.... completed....
for your eyes to see.... My peace.... joy.... prosperity.

The light of My eyes it is yours.
Remember ...I Am the great...I Am.....
The God who sees.

The power and love.... of My light.
The power and love ...of My Beloved
Son, Yeshua Hamaschiack,
Will nurture your body and soul....
With no rest through the day.... through the night.

I Am the great I Am who I Am.
The one who sent you My great light.... for you...
to see and believe.
I Am the one who sees it all.
I created you.... My eyes see.... throughout
the midst of your hearts.
Nowhere to run...or hide.
I follow all of you....
with great mercy and compassion....
I follow you...with great judgment.

I Am the one who will condemn the eyes of the wicked...
the ones who...... will never repent....
the ones who bow to the gods of the flesh....

the ones who keep alive pride in the heart...
the ones who refuse to see Me.

Light that was given to shine their path...light that comes
from the heavens.... from the heart of Great Adonai.
Light that was sent to purify all human kind.

My eyes will see the end of their last breath....
where.... into the fire that never ceases to burn....
by My command, they will be sent......
with great sorrow........into the living dark forever.

The great God who sees is giving you
a chance to see the light....
the great light of salvation .... I send to you....
for you to be redeemed by
My beloved Son....Yeshua Hamaschiack...
the light of the world.

My child, I see the desire of your heart
to make My eyes tear with joy.!
I see you in the midst...looking at My light.

I Am the God who sees your obedient and humble hearts.
I will restore it all .... all that was taken from you....
I will restore your lives with complete peace....
I will restore your eyes...I will give you sight...
for you to see....
The eyes of Great Adonai and salvation for all human kind.

Come to the light My child.... come to Me.....Yeshua the light.
My light was given to you for eternity....as a gift from
Great Adonai.......the day that I died...for you to have...
eternal life .... eternal light....in the sight of My eyes.

My Heart Never Left

Rest in My presence.... I Am here with you....
As your heart beat arises for My presence in you.
As I dwell in the beauty of you.

My heart beat calling you, I feel, I know
it's you ...Yeshua my king!!

I live in you.... your steps following Me I see...
My joy it is yours My child....

I Am ...King Yeshua, Jesus .....My decree it is....
To believe in Me....trust in Me.

Can you feel the breeze ...touching you with kindness?
It was sent from Me....so to love you My child.
As you love My creation...as you think of Me every
time you look around...your eyes I see from above.

Believe and believe...keep trusting in Me.
For I Am .... Yeshua, Jesus the King of My people.
My land and its beauty.... bless forever more....
I dwell in My bride.

My heart and My land....
My heart never left......
My love never left....
My dwelling place is......My love is....in all people's hearts.

My love fulfilled My word....
the great temple will always be.....
My heart never left ....as I walked My
land with you every day.

I heal My people.... I deliver My promises....
through the deliverer, the one who lives in your heart.
My heart never left My land.

As the gentleness of My love is for you....
watch My beloved land.... watch for My signs of love....
for the time, it is coming....to fulfill My
Father's commandments.

The streets will shine.... the great temple will be lit up.

With white wings, I will come....to take place....
To embrace My covenant of love.

My land ...that My heart never left....
with trumpets.... My angels will announce...
The coming of the King.

My Father Great Adonai....will declare...
will proclaim the end.
Finally, you will see.... the glory of the King....for eternity.

The heavens will be opened for the
great day.... the great dance.

Wait for Me....My beloved people....in victory I will return
to the place where My heart never left.

For you who believe and obey.... the beauty of My heart
I left with you.
The beauty of eternal love...that will take you to the promises
I died for.

Only you with purity of heart.... will see the King coming.
to love and restore....
your flesh I will command to perish with
grace....as My love will take place in an
eternal giving.... eternal joy.... eternal peace.... eternal love....
never felt before...My promises will be fulfilled.

Tell others ...My heart never left....to believe in Me....
Yeshua, Jesus the king.
Tell and tell My Fathers spoken words of love.
Tell the great beloved Father....He waiting for your heart....
to believe in Mine.

Obey and obey.... My Fathers decrees....
His mercy endures forever....
His endless love for you awaits.

The eyes of the ones who choose to see...will be blessed...
The eyes of the ones who choose to be blind...
will be condemned.... will in the dark remain....
as they will only be able to feel the wrath of
My heavenly fire.

Tell others the fear.... of Great Adonai will set them free.
Save others...with My sign of love.
Tell others about My endless love.
My heart never left My land as a sign of the story of Love.
As for you My beloved.... I see you from My throne....
I see you with eyes of mercy....I see you with eyes of justice....
I see you with eyes of joy.... I see you with eyes of love.

Wait for Me My beloved...My land it's yours....
My heart I left for you....
Wait for the day of My return.

Keep praying and believing.... keep on saving others....
keep My commandments of love....
keep your eyes on Me.
For I Am Yeshua, Jesus....and only
through the King of Israel....
The King whose heart never left.
All your dreams will be fulfilled forever.

For I Am.....the great King of Israel....
For I Am the King who saves your hearts....

The King who's heart never left the land.
The King who's heart never left yours.

I Am Yeshua, Jesus the king above all!

Everlasting El Olam — Elohim

The light through clouds ...as a sign of
My presence in your heart...
confirmation of My spoken words....
Keep on believing ...that I Am using
your hands to tell of My love.

Jew and gentile......My body will be fulfilled when one
becomes a new life.
Jew and gentile....one path alone....one heart alone....
to glorify My sacrifice.
Jew and gentile.... heart and peace.... past and present....
Everlasting One.

My chosen ones...My loved ones.... are all.
My everlasting lineage with the Israelites.
My land dwells in the past, present and what is to come....
it is not forgotten...it is alive and lives forevermore.

My covenant it is for all.... My heart it is for all.... My
covenant it is with all My people.... My land it is for all.

I... that I Am, Jew and Gentile....
I belong to the future...present and past.
Follow My Holy Sabbath....follow My word.... follow the past.

Believe in the past for ...I Am ...there.
Do not change My law.... the mystery of every word...every act...

every sign... every symbol.... every
living time.... every custom......
with a reason.
Every breath I took.... every breath of My heart...
Everlasting is.
A command for you to follow.......
to understand the love of Hashem.

Do not change My past.... the mystery of My love...
It is given...it is written.
Follow Me... follow the past with devotion in your heart.
Holy scrolls that carry the secrets of My Everlasting love.

Deep inside ...I Am...in everyone.
As there is a sign for you to find.

Refuse to change the past.... the
meaning was already lost once.
Tell others....... of My spoken words.
Tell others .... of My living in the land.
Above all...follow My life the way it was....
as I did live in simpleness.... live with My law....
live dwelling in the scrolls as your most precious possession.

In reverence cover your head......
as I did.
Cleanse your hands before Me...
Cleanse your hearts before the holiness of Hashem,
Before ...Yeshua, Jesus ...the King.

Pray with your heart to the ground....as a reverence to the....
Almighty Father...for mercy will come.

Sanctify your souls.... before you come to Me...
So, that ...I, Yeshua, Jesus will cleanse you before
the glory and majesty
of Great Adonai eternal.

For I Am Yeshua, Jesus....in both Jew and gentile....
I Am Yeshua, Jesus....the King son....
The living everlasting,
El Olam
I Am your past.... Present.
I Am waiting.... for you in the future to find...
that My love is Eternal and Everlasting.

.

A covenant written....in the sacred scrolls...
of your life with the love
of My Everlasting spoken words....
.... Everlasting heart...dwelling in the past...!!

God used the letter "hey" to create the present
God used the letter "yod" for the world to come...!

YHVH

Trials of Love, Trials of Faith

Why My child ....why do you struggle.......when it's Me
who sets you free?
Trials I Am giving you.... for you to learn true love....
For you to know.... that your heart is to be in Me.

The transformation must be complete....
until your heart is complete.
I see the weakness in you....so I come with trials of love.

I know of your human heart.... your flesh
prevails over the spirit in times of trial.
Come to Me....trust in Me.

Lord I did call upon you.......I was lost in fear....

My child you did call upon Me....I heard you calling Me..
but your heart was already apart...away from Me.

Trials come from Me, but no trust...no faith
it is what destroys your heart.
When trials come.......kneel in reverence....
pray with fire in your heart.
Humble yourself to Me.....rather than running away from Me.

Trials are sent from Me to you.... for you to be closer to Me...
and not doubt.

Knowing that.... I Am....behind the scenes ...waiting
for you to learn by trusting in Me.
Trials of love ...trials of faith...will only
be endured.... when in Me.
I Am forming your hearts......until you will be
as the Great Potter has designed.

So, what to do My lord........when suddenly the unknown
comes and we feel like the world stops, the heart stops.?

Pray and pray.... I will give you the wisdom to know....
I will give you the peace to act upon......I will give
you the tenderness for you to understand....
that it is My will.... that will prevail.......
in every situation I bring upon.

I need your heart to be complete.... until then....
learn from Me.....feel My heart.... know My
heart....as it was written in the scrolls.
Every trial that came to Me from above.... I did receive
in the name of love.
Every trial that came from the throne....to this heart of Mine
was formed with endless compassion....
and tenderness for all My people.

My eyes see you with endless love.... for
I know of your imperfection.

I know of your brokenness.... I know of your
weakness.... I know of your wickedness.

My heart was made perfect...so that I will come to you...
and dwell in you.....
and bring you to a place in which your
imperfection....and My heart will be one.

Trials of love.... trials of faith......will be endured
by complete surrender and humility.
Surrender that will open the door to
understanding the Potters will...not yours.

Surrender and let go of your imperfection....
open the door to love, kindness, and
compassion and not judgment.
Compassion that will allow your heart
to love as I did....at the cross...
for that trial of love, I did endure with humility....
with surrender for you My beloved people.

The day of the trial.... (sigh)....in which My heart
was traded for a piece of silver and gold.
Pray and pray.... from the heart......go into your prayer shall,
surrender to Me....leave your pride .... leave
your doubts.... they do not belong to Me.

Be in complete humility.... you will have My heart
and directions and as you do, My beloved,
I will be with you.... working and shaping your own heart.

Be in complete thankfulness......for every trial and
sudden situations.... you will be fulfilled with Me.

You must let Me shape your heart... as
I bring trials of love and faith....
I rejoice ...the heavens rejoice....
as you realize.... that it is Me... shaping you....
for you to shape the heart of My people.

For on the day of the Kingdom....I will know of your heart...
For....I Am... the one who will keep it alive.
See the trials as a chance to be closer to Me....
be of an open heart.... know that it is Me.....
Yeshua, Jesus......that commands in you.

Know that if you choose to refuse to open your
heart and let Me be the potter in your life,
the day of the kingdom, I will know of your heart....
then I will turn away from you as you denied.....
the wisdom I Am given you to understand
that I Am the way, the only way.

My love for you it is beyond your understanding.

I Am teaching you .... teachings from the throne.......
teachings from the heart......
teachings from My word and My own life.

Trials of Love....Trials of Faith......that
comes from the Potter's Heart.

AT the End of the Road

At the end of the road.
Where there is no hope.......Yeshua, Jesus....there is You.
Where there is no grace.... Yeshua, Jesus .... there is You.
Where there is no light........Yeshua, Jesus....there is You.

At the end of the road ....as we see the cliff.... there is You.
At the end of the rope....it is Your holy hand we see.
At the end, it is You ......Yeshua, Jesus our King.
Waiting for us with...... arms wide open.

At the end.... when sickness comes upon.
At the end when the old only sees the end of the road.
At the end of the road were the soldier sees the enemy attack.
At the end.... of the road for every broken
heart......that bleeds out the last hope.
At the end ...were it seems to be the last breath.

It is You Yeshua, Jesus the healer of all human
kind....... that is waiting for us....
with open arms........an eternal shalom.

As I Am answering you while you write,
My arms are open wide.
Since I came to you as a child, My arms were open wide.
As I glorified the Father, My arms were opened wide.
As I took sin, at the cross, from all who would believe,

My arms were open wide.
As I rose to the Father My arms were raised to heaven
where the Fathers arms were open wide too receive Me.

At the end of the road........I Am.....
for all and each of you.........My sweet children.

Run to Me.......run to Me.......
I Am the peace that surpasses your understanding....
your human life.

Why do you choose struggle......if you know about Me...?
The king who came in the name of the Father's love........
Great Adonai........to be with you on the road.

When your hope is gone......come to Me...
I will give you the peace you need ....to continue your walk...
for the road, you must walk....as I did.

The road it is ahead........seek for Me in the midst...
As I walked up the road with the cross.
As I carried your sins........as I carry your dreams.
My eyes were not........ on the hills........
or the crowds beside Me.....
My eyes were upon the Father....
seeing the end of the journey....
The Father had prepared for Me........for you to be in Me.

Follow Me....My child......do not stop and do not seek
what is not of Me....
Keep on walking the path I wrote for you on the scrolls.
The path of the cross........the stones you will feel....as I did.
Denial you will feel as you speak of Me.......
My walk with the cross.... a place of love...a place of hate....
where I dwelt.

As I did......with great obedience.
see the love of the great Father.... keep
on trusting in My word.

The word...the law ...it is your shield...
My love it is your sword.
My blood it is covering ...as you walk and follow Me.

Under your tallit, you will find atonement........
As you learn to repent of your ...thoughts...actions...words.
As you bring your heart in completion
and surrender.......to Me.....
For I Am holy.
Your walk then will be shadowed......for I know the end.

Bring My people to Me....Yeshua Hamaschiack....Sar Shalom.
I see their hearts mourning at the wall.... for their King....
mourning for what is to come....
mourning for the past.
They already know Me....
I Am...in them... they are in Me.

Your heart...your hands...will tell of My love....
will tell of My Name ...Yeshua, Jesus the King of the bride ...
King of Jerushalayim.
Will tell them.... that I Am at the end of the road...
Waiting for you...to fulfill the Father's command of love....
Great Adonai ......Great Hashem......YHVH.

My beloved ...I Am your King....Yeshua, Jesus....
The one who came from the great throne ...in obedience....
to prepare the road for you to walk.

Search for Me on the road.......for I Am there....
only if you choose to see My endless love.
Come and walk with Me.....
to the land, I have prepared for you.

My kingdom it is yours....My love it is dwelling in you...
now and forevermore...until the very end...
until the road it is fulfilled with My
word and all your dreams.

I Am with you always.....I Am ...the Son of the Great King.

Yeshua Hamaschiack, Jesus the Messiah....
The one at the beginning of the road....
the one at the end of the road......waiting for you My child....
with eternal, Shalom.

With My Arms Open Wide!

A PRAYER FROM THE WRITER

So, I pray and so I love.

I pray to you my Love, my Lord. I pray with a humble heart, with my feet uncovered, for it is holy ground under my tallit.

Pray to You for mercy, that You my King will find purity and humbleness of heart in me.

So, that through you my King Yeshua, Jesus my prayers will be transformed into whispers of love to YHVH, our Father in heaven.

Amen.

His Answer:

Be in Me ......be prepared....
I AM coming to judge the living and the dead......
I AM coming to the end, that is near.
The prayers of the saints I hear.
The prayers of My people I hear.

Prepare .... pray when you come before Me in surrender, in redemption.

For the time is near......

The power of prayer .... the power of heaven....

the power of love ....the power of hate.

Angels and demons at war.

The Sword ...the Seals ...all will be by the Fathers Law.

The known and the unknown.

The heart of man aligns with the truth.... aligns with lies.

The great battle, the last dance.

I YESHUA, JESUS the Son of the Great I AM.......

will come in the midst of the great mist.

The heart of man, the heart of the beast will tremble, will surrender.

This earth of Mine that I once walked in the midst of peace, in the midst of war.

Will see the returning of the King.

All that is known and unknown will be revealed.

Life and death will be in an instant.

The Breath of great HASHEM the Breath of life and death will be again as

it was in the beginning of creation.

Your prayers are heard for they are in My heart.

The purity of your love will be saved.

So, pray from the heart.... know of your enemy and follow your King.

For on the day of the sword I will be with you, in prayer

as I did pray to My Father in heaven with tears of blood at the time that had to be done.

The time of the cross.

So, pray and pray, for the Father knows the true heart....

truth that will be transformed unto whispers of love.

The Great Father is pleased when a prayer is placed as an offering.

Your tears become as an incense of sweet aroma for the Father's merciful heart.

Your mourning hearts are the prayers of the saints.

The prayers of the wicked will not be heard.

I will destroy.... I will condemn.

The prayer of the saints I will answer.

My angels are charged, ready to come and lift you up on the day of the great battle they will be with you, their wings will be wrapped around you, to protect your prayerful hearts.

So, the battle will go on.... your prayers will be in the battlefield as your most precious shield....

I listen to your prayers ...I love your praying hearts.

Do not give up ...do not be afraid.... for the end, you will see.

Every time you kneel your heart into the ground...and pray to Me in truth.

I ...will make you strong...I will give you wisdom.... I will cleanse your heart so that

your prayer will become whispers of love to great ADONAI.

I AM preparing you with love and tenderness...I AM using your tears to intercede for all human kind.

So, pray and follow My commands ....in truth ...in love.

Truly, I Yeshua, Jesus the Son of The Great I AM, will honor your desire and your prayers will be heard as whispers of love to the Father who sits

On the Heaven's Throne.

~ GOY ~

* * *

To the Nations

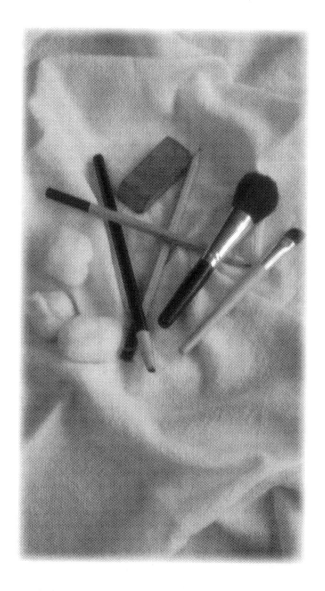

Simple tools used to create the drawings:
Pencils, erasers, cotton balls and make up brushes.

Printed in the United States
By Bookmasters